The Success Formula

ISBN: 978-0-9980369-4-6
LCCN: 2019937325

Most CelebrityPress® titles are available at special quantity discounts for bulk purchases for sales promotions, premiums, fundraising, and educational use. Special versions or book excerpts can also be created to fit specific needs.

For more information, please write:
CelebrityPress®
520 N. Orlando Ave, #2
Winter Park, FL 32789
or call 1.877.261.4930

Visit us online at: www.CelebrityPressPublishing.com

The Success Formula

CelebrityPress®
Winter Park, Florida

CONTENTS

CHAPTER 1

AN EFFECTIVE SYSTEM FOR ACHIEVING SUCCESS

BY JACK CANFIELD

One of the biggest myths in the world today is that, in order to achieve success, you must be smart enough, educated enough, or wealthy enough—with the right ideas, connections, and timing—in order to reach your goals and achieve the lifestyle of your dreams. But the reality is that these arbitrary requirements simply aren't needed.

What's needed is the right formula.

When I first conceived the book idea that eventually became my bestselling *Chicken Soup for the Soul*® series, I was simply responding to interest from my students, audiences and clients. Day after day, as I spoke at business conferences, education conferences and local civic events, I always included true stories of ordinary people who had found the courage to go for their dreams, had overcome adversity, and had made a difference in the lives of others, to illustrate the effectiveness of the principles I was teaching. Everywhere I spoke people would come up to me afterwards and ask, "Are those stories you told in a book anywhere?"

After hearing this same question day after day, I eventually realized that these stories were not just teaching people valuable lessons, they were also uplifting their spirit as well. They were transforming them into individuals who were more inspired, motivated, thoughtful, and kind.

But these inspirational and heart-warming stories were just one ingredient in making *Chicken Soup for the Soul* the monumental success it became. For the next two years, as I collected stories with my coauthor Mark Victor Hansen and my office manager Patty Aubery, we wrote and edited the book multiple times, hired a literary agent, and eventually found a publisher (after being turned down 144 times over a fourteen month period). Just as important as these actions was the internal work we were doing – we continued to believe in ourselves, be persistent, and listened to and trusted our intuition.

These combined elements eventually produced what has become the most published non-fiction book series of all time with more than 230 titles and more than 500 million books sold in forty-nine languages around the world.

Was it easy? No. Did it take hard work? Yes. But what we honed and refined in the process is a formula for success that can be replicated in any endeavor that you choose to pursue in your own life.

Whether it's changing careers, starting a new charity, writing a book, launching a new product, winning a major award or growing your own business, you can use the same formula to create the same kind of success.

INGREDIENT #1:
DECIDE WHAT YOU WANT TO DO, BE AND HAVE

One of the most amazing phenomenon you'll ever experience as you pursue success is the unexpected phone call, the windfall financial benefit or the uncanny new acquaintance that brings you exactly what you want or need in order to achieve your loftiest goals—almost as if it were planned.

Perhaps it's the Universe rewarding your new goal-setting activity and take-action attitude by harnessing all the forces at its disposal. Or perhaps you've worked hard and have "grown" yourself to the point where you're finally ready to receive a benefit which had been waiting in the wings all along.

But most likely, as researchers have now come to believe, it may simply be a matter of your subconscious mind focusing on and recognizing opportunity when it arrives. Whatever the explanation, the reality is that what you want, wants you. Your goals, desires and needs are patiently waiting to gravitate toward you, once you decide what you truly want.

Of course, the main reason why most people don't get what they want is they haven't clearly and unambiguously decided what they truly want. They haven't defined their goals in clear and compelling detail. Once you clearly decide what you want, your subconscious mind begins to work on figuring out how to achieve it. Your clear decision of what you want also programs your brain to start perceiving all the resources—both internal and external—that can help you reach your goal.

Clarify Your Vision and Your Values

There's a very powerful technique for helping you define your goals in vivid, colorful and compelling detail. But before using this technique to write down your goals—before defining the compelling life you want for yourself, you first must know what your priorities are. Priorities are "wants" that are personally important to you—not those you believe should be important or those you believe the world expects you to value—but what's truly important to you from the deepest place in your heart.

Once you know your "wants," you must also determine your core values. What kinds of activities and priorities are in alignment with your values, your ethics, and your integrity? And which are outside your acceptable limits?

Think about it. You might "want" all the riches and material wealth that could come from selling illegal drugs, but you might find it very difficult to convince your mind and body of your enthusiasm, especially if breaking the law and contributing to broken lives went against your basic values. In fact, engaging in an activity you don't agree with often causes low self-esteem, depression, despondency, even anger. So be sure that what you want matches your values and your understanding of your life purpose.

Don't Live Someone Else's Dream

Be certain, too, that what you "want" isn't someone else's version of what you should want.

I once worked with an anesthesiologist who made $350,000 a year, but who was not happy and was suffering from chronic pain. His real dream was to work on cars. He had wanted to be a mechanic, but he knew his family, all of whom were doctors, wouldn't approve. The result of not living his dream was that he constantly had migraine headaches and back pain. What his heart wanted and what his "shoulds" were didn't match.

After coaching with me, he gave himself permission to buy a few older cars and rebuild them on the weekends. Eventually he quit his medical career and opened a garage where he upgraded luxury cars into high performance racecars. Unfortunately, the sad reality for most people is they simply aren't honest with themselves. If they were, they would realize their true "wants" are always more important and more fulfilling than their "shoulds" will ever be.

Visualize What You Want

To create a checklist of what you want to be, do and have, use the following exercise. You can either audio-record the instructions yourself, then play them back during the exercise, or you can have a friend read the instructions to you.

Begin by putting on some relaxing instrumental music (without words) and sitting quietly in a comfortable environment. Close your eyes and take six slow relaxing breaths. Then, begin visualizing each of the following areas of your ideal life exactly as you would like it to be with no constrictions and without worrying how you would actually create it. Just create the way you would like it if you knew you could have anything you want. Take as much time as you need with each question.

1. First, visualize your financial situation. How much money do you have in your savings? What is your annual income? What is your net worth? If you own a business, how is your cash flow? What does your home look like? Where is it located? What color are the walls? Are there paintings or other artwork hanging on the walls? What do they look like? What kind of furniture do you have? Walk through your perfect house visually, using your mind's eye.

   At this point, don't worry about how you'll get that house. Don't sabotage yourself by saying, "I can't live in Malibu because I don't make enough money." Once you give your mind's eye the picture, your mind will solve the "not enough money" challenge.

   Simply be honest with yourself about what you truly want. Continue visualizing your perfect home. Next, visualize what kind of car you are driving.

2. Next, visualize your ideal job or career. What are you doing in your career? Where are you working? Who are you

working with? What kinds of projects are you working on? What kinds of coworkers or employees do you have? What kind of clients or customers do you have? Do you own your own business?

3. Then focus on your free time, your recreation time, what you do for fun. What are you doing with your family and friends in the free time you've created for yourself? What hobbies are you pursuing? What kinds of vacations do you take?

4. Next, visualize your body and your physical health, your emotional and spiritual life. Are you free and open? Are you calm and relaxed? Are you strong and flexible? Are you at your ideal weight? Are you healthy and pain free? Are you happy all day long?

5. Then move on to visualizing your relationships with your family and friends. What is your relationship with your family like? Who are your friends? What is the quality of your relationships with your friends? What do those friendships feel like? Are they loving, nurturing, supportive and empowering?

6. What about your personal growth? Do you see yourself going back to school, getting more training, taking workshops, working with a coach, engaging in individual therapy or couples counseling? Are you growing spiritually with a teacher or as part of a spiritual community?

7. Now focus on the community you live in, the community you've chosen. What does your ideal community look and feel like? What kinds of community activities take place there? Are you engaged in any charitable or philanthropic work? What do you do to make a difference in the lives of others? How often do you participate in these activities? Who are you helping?

Once you complete this exercise, take the time to write out in detail your ideal vision for each area of your life. Next, take each area of your vision and turn it into specific and measurable goals with a date by which you want to have it. Don't worry about the how; just write down each goal. The mere act of writing each part of your vision as a concrete, measurable goal with a deadline has a magical effect on your ability to achieve that goal. Research has shown that just writing the goal down rather than simply thinking about it in your head increases your chances of achieving it by 17%.

When Mark and I published *Chicken Soup for the Soul*, we set the goal to sell 150,000 copies by Christmas of that year and a million and a half copies in a year and a half. We outperformed everyone else's expectations by selling 135,000 copies by Christmas and 1.3 million in a year and a half. Our publisher had originally laughed at us and told us we would be lucky to sell 20,000!

INGREDIENT #2:
FIND MENTORS WHO CAN HELP YOU

Most people tend to ask their friends, neighbors, co-workers and siblings for advice on key issues they may be facing in their life. Too often, they ask the advice of others who have never triumphed over a specific hardship or never succeeded in the specific area you're working on.

Perhaps this describes you.

An alternative way to get answers and advice is to find a wing to climb under—or three or four.

Surround yourself with advisors, mentors, experts and friends who have succeeded in the specific tasks or skills you need to be good at.

Approach them and ask for help...and then do what they tell you to do.

While it may seem daunting at first to reach out and contact successful people and ask them for ongoing advice and assistance, it's actually easier than you think to enlist the mentorship of those who have gone before you in the areas you'd like to succeed in.

When Mark and I published *Chicken Soup for the Soul*, we reached out to seven best-selling authors like John Gray (*Men Are from Mars, Women Are from Venus*) and Ken Blanchard (*The One Minute Manager*) and asked for their advice. All seven of these authors gave us their time and their advice, which was extremely helpful and allowed us to achieve our goal much faster than we would have without it.

First, Do Your Homework

One of the key strategies for getting people to say yes is to ask the right person and ask in the right way. In other words, give all the reasons why you are asking *them* and tell them what you'll do with any assistance you're given.

It's no different with approaching potential mentors. This means you must do your homework—first, in order to develop your list of possible mentors, but secondly, so you'll know specifically what to ask for when you get them on the phone.

One of the easiest ways to research the names and backgrounds of people who have been successful in your area of interest is to read industry magazines, search the Internet, ask trade association Executive Directors, attend trade shows and conventions, call fellow entrepreneurs or approach others who operate in industry, profession or area of interest.

Look for mentors who have the kind of well-rounded experience you need to learn about to tackle your goal. When you start seeing a pattern of the same few people being recommended, you'll know you've identified your possible mentors.

INGREDIENT #3:
DEVELOP HABITS THAT
WILL PROPEL YOU TO SUCCESS

Many of our daily activities are simply routine. From the time you get up in the morning until you retire at night, there are hundreds of things you do the same way. These include the way you dress, get ready for the day, eat breakfast, read the newspaper, brush your teeth, drive to the office, greet people, arrange your desk, set up appointments, work on projects, attend meetings, answer the phone and so on.

If you've been doing these same activities for years, you have developed a set of firmly entrenched habits. They involve every area of your life including your work, family, income, health, relationships and many more. The sum total of these habits determines how your life operates.

Simply stated, this has become your normal behavior.

How Habits Really Work

So, what is a habit? Simply stated, a habit is something you do so often it becomes automatic and easy. In other words, it's a behavior that you keep repeating. If you persist at developing a new behavior, eventually it too becomes an automatic habit.

When you're developing a new habit, you want to use a "no exceptions policy". In other words, you commit to your new habit every single day no matter what. This level of commitment is what separates the people who are successful in life from the people who are not successful.

Say maintaining excellent health is high on your list of priorities.

Then exercising three times a week may be the minimum standard to keep you in shape. A No Exceptions Policy means you will maintain this exercise habit no matter what happens (rain, snow, travel, house guests, etc.), because you value the long-term benefits in terms of energy, strength, stamina, and longevity. People who simply dabble at change will quit after a few weeks or months. And they usually have a long list of excuses why it didn't work out for them.

If you want to distance yourself from the masses and enjoy the benefits of a unique, prosperous lifestyle, understand this—your habits will determine your future. It's that important. Remember, successful people don't drift to the top. It takes focused action, personal discipline and lots of energy every day to make things happen. The habits you develop from this day forward will ultimately determine how your future works out.

Good or Bad, Habits Always Deliver Results

One of the problems in life is that the results of your bad habits usually don't show up until much later in life.

When you develop a chronic bad habit, life will eventually give you consequences. And you may not like those consequences. Here's what you need to really understand: Life will still give you the consequences. Whether you like it or not isn't the issue. The fact is, if you keep on doing things a certain way, you will always get a predictable result. Negative habits breed negative consequences. Successful habits create positive rewards.

How To Start Changing Your Habits

Developing successful habits takes time. In fact, recent scientific studies put the estimated time at about 60 to 66 days to develop a new habit. But before you change a habit, you need to first check how long you have owned it. If you have been doing something repeatedly for thirty years, you may not be able to let go of it in a few short weeks. Acknowledge the fact that a deeply entrenched habit has long roots. It's like trying to sever a multi-stranded fiber that has molded itself over time, into a single powerful rope. It's very hard to break. Long-time smokers know how difficult it is to break the nicotine habit. Many never do, despite the overwhelming evidence that proves smoking can significantly shorten your life expectancy.

Similarly, people with a long history of low self-esteem won't transform themselves into highly confident individuals, ready to take on the world, in twenty-one days. It may take months or even a year to develop more positive belief systems. However, committing to do the work to change your habitual thinking and behavioral habits can have a huge impact on both your professional and personal life.

Another factor about changing habits is the potential for slipping back into your old patterns. This can happen when stress levels rise or an unexpected crisis occurs. The new habit may not be strong enough to resist these circumstances, and more time, energy and effort will be required. To ensure consistency, pilots and astronauts use a checklist for every single procedure they do in order to ensure the same results every time. You can also create a similar fail-safe system. It just takes a checklist or a method for keeping score and practice. And it's well worth the effort, as you'll see shortly.

Imagine if you only changed four habits a year (one every quarter). Five years from now you'd have twenty positive new habits. Now, here's the thing—would twenty positive new habits make a difference in your results? Of course! Twenty successful habits can bring you all the money you want or need, wonderful loving relationships, a healthier more energized physical body, plus all sorts of new opportunities. And what if you created more than four new habits a year? Think of the possibilities!

When Mark and I released *Chicken Soup for the Soul*, we

developed two new habits that we learned from our mentors. The first was to do three radio interviews a day for the first year and then one a day for the next three years. The second was to use the "Rule of 5", which is to take five small actions every day toward the achievement of your number one goal, which at that time was to get our book onto the New York Times bestseller list. It took us fourteen months to get on the list, but once we got there, we stayed there for three years. Other new habits we developed were to meditate for twenty minutes every day, read for an hour a day, and exercise for a minimum of twenty minutes a day.

By systematically adding one new habit at a time, you can dramatically improve every area of your life.

Take Action to Change Your Habits Now

There are two action steps for changing your habits. The first is to make a list of all the habits you have that keep you unproductive. Make sure to block out an hour or more for this so you can really think through this process. Until you clearly understand what is holding you back, it's difficult to create new, more productive habits. The most common bad work habits include:

- Not returning phone calls on time
- Being late for meetings and appointments
- Not attending to paperwork quickly and efficiently
- Texting during phone calls, meetings or in social settings
- Not following up on overdue receivables
- Talking instead of listening
- Forgetting someone's name sixty seconds or less after being introduced
- Working long days with no exercise or breaks
- Not spending enough time with your children
- Having fast-food meals Monday through Friday
- Making reservations at the last minute
- Procrastinating on everything from filing your taxes to cleaning out your garage

Another way to identify your unproductive habits is to ask for feedback. Talk to people you respect and admire and who know you well. Ask them what they observe about your bad habits. Look for consistency. If you talk to ten people and eight of them say you never return phone calls on time, pay attention. Remember this—your outward behavior is the truth, whereas your inner perception of your behavior is often an illusion.

Creating New Habits That Support Your Success

Once you make a list of your unproductive habits, the second step is to change your bad habits into good ones using this formula:

1. **Clearly identify your bad or unproductive habits**. Think about the future consequences of your bad habits. These may not show up until tomorrow, next week or next month. In fact, the real impact could be years away. So when you examine your own bad habits, consider the long-term implications. Be honest with yourself. Your very life could be at stake.

2. **Define one new successful habit at a time to work on**. Usually just the opposite of your bad habit, your new successful habit is one you should decide what you *will do* versus what you won't do. For example, a smoker might say his or her new successful habit will be to *stop* smoking. That won't work. You need to determine what you *will do*, not just what you *won't do*. What specific actions will you take in order to stop smoking? Will you see a doctor? Wear the patch? Chew gum? Work with a hypnotist or self-hypnosis tapes? Use the EFT tapping techniques to rid the cravings? Also, to motivate yourself, make sure to identify and constantly remind yourself of all the benefits and rewards for adopting your new successful habit—like better health, money saved, living cancer free and living longer. This helps you create a clear picture of what this new habit will do for you. The more vividly you describe the benefits, the more likely you are to take action.

3. **Create an action plan for the one new habit.** Focus on three immediate action steps that will help you achieve the new habit, then put them into practice. For example, if you work long hours at a desk without breaks or exercise, your action plan might be to: (1) set your smartphone alarm to alert you once every hour to get up and move around, (2) identify a park a half-mile away that you can walk to at lunchtime, and (3) get a hands-free headset so you can walk around during lengthy conference calls. Create your action plan now. And remember, nothing will change for the better until you do.

THE FINAL INGREDIENT:
WHEN YOU TAKE ACTION, GO THE EXTRA MILE

In his timeless classic *Think and Grow Rich*, Napoleon Hill writes: *The main trouble with so many of us is that we see men who have "arrived," and we weigh them in the hour of their triumph without taking the trouble to find out how or why they arrived.*

The truth is that most of the "overnight" success stories you read about are really the result of decades of hard work, years of extra effort and a lifetime of perseverance.

These people are often over-achievers—who simply aren't satisfied with "good enough," but who seek out opportunities to deliver more, to provide extra value, to produce 110% and to do a better job.

They are people who go the extra mile.

Almost by force of habit, successful people simply do more. Not surprisingly, this "do more" habit actually helps create new possibilities in their lives, because they're constantly placed in the way of ever-greater opportunity. Imagine what would happen to you if you stayed just fifteen minutes longer after the rest of your fellow employees left for the day...or what you could accomplish if you took charge of some activity that was languishing from lack of manpower. Are there circumstances in your life right now where you could do more, provide better value, over-deliver or improve upon what is asked of you?

Do you have the opportunity—but also the personal initiative—to go the extra mile?

The Big Payoff: Why Would Anyone Want to Go the Extra Mile?

Consider the two most important reasons for going the extra mile: (1) You experience greater rewards for your efforts, at the same time becoming more valuable to your employers, customers and clients. (2) You experience a personal transformation, becoming more confident, more self-reliant, more enthusiastic, and more influential with those around you...all traits of successful people.

So, what's the pay-off for you? What can you expect from going the extra mile? Surprisingly, most rewards are unexpected...a surprise promotion, an unusual bonus, a greater area of responsibility, or unusually lucrative revenues for your business. But you have to start in order for the rewards to appear.

Make a commitment to go the extra mile every day for a month and notice the results. I promise you'll be surprised.

About Jack

Known as America's #1 Success Coach, Jack Canfield is the CEO of the Canfield Training Group in Santa Barbara, CA, which trains and coaches entrepreneurs, corporate leaders, managers, sales professionals and the general public in how to accelerate the achievement of their personal, professional and financial goals.

Jack Canfield is best known as the coauthor of the #1 *New York Times* bestselling *Chicken Soup for the Soul®* book series, which has sold more than 500 million books in 47 languages, including 11 *New York Times* #1 bestsellers. As the CEO of Chicken Soup for the Soul Enterprises he helped grow the *Chicken Soup for the Soul®* brand into a virtual empire of books, children's books, audios, videos, CDs, classroom materials, a syndicated column and a television show, as well as a vigorous program of licensed products that includes everything from clothing and board games to nutraceuticals and a successful line of *Chicken Soup for the Pet Lover's Soul®* cat and dog foods.

His other books include *The Success Principles™: How to Get from Where You Are to Where You Want to Be* (recently revised as the 10th Anniversary Edition), *The Success Principles for Teens, The Aladdin Factor, Dare to Win, Heart at Work, The Power of Focus: How to Hit Your Personal, Financial and Business Goals with Absolute Certainty, You've Got to Read This Book, Tapping into Ultimate Success, Jack Canfield's Key to Living the Law of Attraction,* his recent novel, *The Golden Motorcycle Gang: A Story of Transformation and The 30-Day Sobriety Solution.*

Jack is a dynamic speaker and was recently inducted into the National Speakers Association's Speakers Hall of Fame. He has appeared on more than 1000 radio and television shows including Oprah, Montel, Larry King Live, the Today Show, Fox and Friends, and 2 hour-long PBS Specials devoted exclusively to his work. Jack is also a featured teacher in 12 movies including *The Secret, The Meta-Secret, The Truth, The Keeper of the Keys, Tapping into the Source,* and *The Tapping Solution.* Jack was also honored recently with a documentary that was produced about his life and teachings, *The Soul of Success: The Jack Canfield Story.*

Jack has personally helped hundreds of thousands of people on six different continents become multi-millionaires, business leaders, best-selling authors, leading sales professionals, successful entrepreneurs, and world-class athletes while at the same time creating balanced, fulfilling and healthy lives.

His corporate clients have included Virgin Records, SONY Pictures, Daimler-Chrysler, Federal Express, GE, Johnson & Johnson, Merrill Lynch, Campbell's Soup, Re/Max, The Million Dollar Forum, The Million Dollar Roundtable, The Young Entrepreneurs Organization, The Young Presidents Organization, the Executive Committee, and the World Business Council.

Jack is the founder of the Transformational Leadership Council and a member of Evolutionary Leaders, two groups devoted to helping create a world that works for everyone.

Jack is a graduate of Harvard, earned his M.Ed. from the University of Massachusetts, and has received three honorary doctorates in psychology and public service. He is married, has three children, two step-children and a grandson.

For more information, visit:
- www.JackCanfield.com
- www.CanfieldTraintheTrainer.com

CHAPTER 2

VALUABLE AND WORTHWHILE

BY DENISE HEALY, MA

I direct a team of Victim's Advocates who work with violent offenders. One day I excitedly shared the work we do with a small group of friends and family. I spoke of the new modalities we are using and how we seamlessly integrate state of the art technology with providing service for the highest at risk in our communities. I shared how the company was growing leaps and bounds and how we are hiring quality staff. I perceived the conversation as positive. Not everyone did.

At the end of the conversation, one person walked away, and I heard him saying, "I don't understand why she wants to work with those people." I was taken aback by this perception and comment. It upset me for a while until I could figure out the best way to communicate the 'why' of it all.

There is an easy, one-line answer to the question as to 'why' I do what I do. The premise of the work is that if an offender can stop being violent, there will be a reduction in victimization. Unless someone is really interested in the work, they do not ask another probing question. Yet, there is a more thorough, complex, dare-I-say fulfilling, answer to satisfy the question as to 'why' I do what I do. It is best illustrated through a story.

I sat with a professional confidant to debrief after a stressful situation I had had with one of my clients. I was struggling with fatigue and was fearful that the work was getting to me in an unhealthy way. I am clear on my purpose and ability to work with the violent offender. But I was questioning the stress of working up close and personal with this population over time. I shared with my confidant the comment I overheard, 'I don't understand why she wants to work with those people' and a difficult phone conversation, with a client.

I started in. I told my friend about how recently a work call was patched through to me. It was during off-hours. No group session was in progress. Clients know that they can call in for support anytime. A young man was calling for help.

"Miss Denise?"

"Yes. This is Denise. How can I help you?"

"I just need someone to actively listen to me."

I smile at the young caller's request. He was referring to the concept we had reviewed in the last group session he attended. I knew he was asking for someone to refrain from judgement, criticism and blame. "Of course, I am here to listen to you. What's going on?"

"I just want you to listen to me, be with me, while I bleed out."

I hit the ground running on actively listening! The caller's fragment of a sentence, 'while I bleed out' gave a strong indication that he was in some sort of danger. I determined there was a high degree of seriousness regarding a threat to his life. I go into action and pick up a secondary cell phone. I text my partner who serves as the operations manager and asks her to begin the triage process. A first responder needed to get to his address to assess the situation immediately. My partner was able to contact his probation officer and the police with the express intent of protecting the caller from further harm. Help was on the way.

Within seconds I said, "I will stay with you and actively listen. I just want you to know I will do my best to see that you do not bleed out today."

The caller began to cry. "I cut myself. About four inches up my wrists. There's a lot of blood." I could hear the fear and panic in his voice.

"So you cut yourself." I paraphrased what he said.

"Yes!" He screeches.

"Do you have two T-shirts or a sheet nearby?" I could hear him moving around and made a mental note. He hasn't lost too much blood given that he still can stand.

"Got two T-shirts right here."

"Good. Wrap one T-shirt around each of your wrists and put pressure on them while we talk."

"Ok. Ok. Ok. I got it."

I shifted the conversation. "So let's practice 'active listening' together, shall we?"

"Ok."

"Can you rephrase what I just asked you to do?"

He followed my lead. "You asked me to get two T-shirts, so I did. Then you told me to wrap the T-shirts around my wrists and put pressure on them." He was calming down. "It does feel better Miss Denise."

"I am grateful you are feeling better."

It took all of twenty minutes for help to reach him. In that time he and I had an extraordinary exchange. We both practiced active listening. Neither of us judged the other. There was no criticism or blame in the conversation. We carried out the exchange through stopping, thinking, and rephrasing each other's thoughts before moving on to our own idea. We acknowledge each other as valuable and worthwhile.

We spoke of his pain and fear. He questioned what it meant to live a purposeful life. He asked me to talk about how he could practice putting love first always. We explored his idea of a personal relationship with God.

When the officers reached the front door of the young man's apartment, he was calm. I stayed on the phone with him until the ambulance and medics arrived. He let himself be cared for and hung up the phone with me only when the medics said it was time to go to the hospital. He did not bleed out that night.

I hung up the phone exhausted. Yet, in those 20 minutes I got to know the young caller in a way I would have never been able to unless we both agreed to practice active listening.

ACTIVE LISTENING

The caller understood the basics of active listening based on the two-hour group session where he learned about the concept. That he asked to practice active listening suggests that he was reaching for a strategy to get himself out of his current situation. That he called for support communicated to me that he really didn't want to die. He wanted to be listened to and connect with someone.

American psychologist Carl Rogers, Ph.D., a founding theorist of humanistic psychology, originated the term "active listening."

Rogers's client-centered therapeutic approach surmised that for people to "grow" and reach self-actualization, they need an environment that provides them with the core conditions of empathy, congruence, and unconditional positive regard.[1]

The "active listening" technique sets the stage for relational growth because it requires a collaborative effort in communication where the listener becomes as active as the speaker. To provide an environment which meets the core conditions of empathy, congruence, and unconditional positive regard for the speaker, the listener must remain actively present. The "active listening" strategy includes the listener acknowledging what he or she has heard by rephrasing and checking for a full understanding of what is being communicated.[2, 3]

To break the technique of active listening down into layman's terms, one needs only to examine the definitions of the two words.

- To be active is to take action or become effective. In a relationship, it just means to be busy, energetic, protective, and to take an interest in someone or something other than one's self.
- Listening is not just hearing. Real listening is the ability to receive and interpret messages that have been communicated accurately.

As the caller and I practiced putting the two ideas together, we were able to conclusively show interest by conscientiously paying attention to whoever was speaking, thereby accurately receiving and interpreting the other's thought or idea before focusing on what we wanted to share.

---

1. On Becoming a Person: A Therapist's View of Psychotherapy. Carl R. Rogers, Houghton Mifflin Company, 1961, 1989, 1995.
2. A Way of Being. Carl R. Rogers, Introduction by Irvin D. Yalom, Houghton Mifflin Company, Sep 7, 1995 reprint of 1980 Edition.
3. Active Listening. Carl R. Rogers and Richard Evans, Martino Publishing, Nov 2015 reprint of 1943 Edition.

Active Listening at Work

Knowing about and understanding how active listening works is far different from applying and using them consistently in real-life situations. The caller learned in two hours all about active listening. It wasn't until he was in a real-life situation that he was able to apply the concept leading to a positive outcome effectively.

For us to successfully accomplish active listening in the communication process, it was essential we consider and practice the following three principles[4]:

1. Refrain from judgment, criticism, or blame.
2. Acknowledge that the other person is valuable and worthwhile.
3. Stop, think, and rephrase a presented idea before moving on to another idea.

Communicate when you are able to be an active listener and when you're not.

1. Refrain from Judgment, Criticism, and Blame

Thoughts travel quickly through our heads during a conversation. Thoughts were indeed rushing around in my head during my conversation with the caller. There were many times when he was talking, and before he finished communicating a complete thought, I formed an opinion about what he was saying. I resisted drawing conclusions before I fully understood what he was attempting to communicate. He and I worked to remain focused on the entire thought or idea that was being conveyed.

I refrained from premature judgment on the topics to avoid unwarranted criticism. I didn't want to assess the merits of what he was saying with unfavorable thoughts and comments.

---

4. Mending Broken Connections: 10 Simple Strategies to Restore Communication in Relationships. Denise Healy, Cedar Rose Publishing, Feb. 2019.

He never found fault with my reasoning and allowed for real connection in the communication. Active listening kept us engaged throughout each other's entire thought process— that is until we really saw each other's point of view. This made for a peaceful conversation.

2. Acknowledge Value and Worthiness

It was vital for me to share my individual points of view in the exchange with the caller. However, it was more important to acknowledge him as valuable and worthwhile. Active listening required me to put the caller and the conversation above all else. To acknowledge him entirely means I must be willing to recognize his truth and what he might be saying. My acknowledgment remained on his person, his value and worthiness to be heard. To be clear, I did not always agree with him. But that did not matter in the conversation. It was more important to accept his right to be heard.

3. Stop, Think, and Rephrase

The three steps of "stop, think, and rephrase" are harder to accomplish than one might think. In the case of my talking to the caller, it was imperative that I directed him to this active listening step. It was essential for him to stop all thoughts and discontinue any distracting behaviors so that I could ascertain that he followed my direction to wrap his wrists in T-shirts and put pressure on the wounds to slow the bleeding. He was able to stop, think, and rephrase what was asked of him. This provided me with a measure of comfort knowing he could remain present for the help.

When I finished sharing the story and looked up at my professional confidant, she was calm, serene, glowing. The comfort of her hand rested on my back. She was quiet for a moment and then shared her thoughts with great confidence.

"I understand why you work with and are around 'those' people."

She said with a soft smile. She let the comment settle in before taking another tack.

We spoke of my state of fatigue and any fear that was associated with the work I do. She and I spoke of my focus on living a purposeful life of service. She reminded me of my practice of putting love first always with family, friends, and those I serve. Finally, we spoke of my personal relationship with God.

In the amount of time it took for first responders to reach the caller my confidant actively listened to me. Both exchanges were equally extraordinary. I did not feel judged, criticized, or blamed. I felt heard and acknowledged as valuable and worthwhile.

"Those people are all people." She said quietly. "We all want to be listened to, we all want to be heard, valued, and considered worthwhile."

References
1. **On Becoming a Person: A Therapist's View of Psychotherapy**. Carl R. Rogers, Houghton Mifflin Company, 1961, 1989, 1995.
2. **A Way of Being**. Carl R. Rogers, Introduction by Irvin D. Yalom, Houghton Mifflin Company, Sep 7, 1995 reprint of 1980 Edition.
3. **Active Listening**. Carl R. Rogers and Richard Evans, Martino Publishing, Nov 2015 reprint of 1943 Edition.
4. **Mending Broken Connections: 10 Simple Strategies to Restore Communication in Relationships**. Denise Healy, Cedar Rose Publishing, Feb. 2019.

[NOTE: Names, characters, places, events, locales, and incidents described herein this chapter are the products of the author's imagination based on a composite of stories and used in a citation manner to more fully illustrate the particular point discussed in the chapter. Any resemblance to actual persons, living or dead, or actual events is purely coincidental.]

About Denise

Denise Healy, MA is privileged to assist and support people who are seeking to better themselves by taking steps to make positive changes in their relationships. She is dedicated to helping those who are seeking a way to reconnect with a loved one and arming them with the positive, social skills they need to bring harmony back into their lives.

Denise has taught, mentored, coached, and counseled literally thousands of people over the last four decades. She is versed in knowing which strategies work to mend broken connections in relationships. Denise adds value to people through assisting them in applying positive social skills strategies to real life circumstances, so as to yield positive outcomes and success. She is invested in building relationships, adding value to teams, and increasing psycho-educational performance outcomes.

Denise is an educator and psychologist. She is a John C. Maxwell Certified Coach and speaker. Her newest venture is as an American author and entrepreneur. Denise established Cedar Rose Publishing. She embarked on this journey to further support non-fiction and historical fiction work in the areas of education and psychology. Denise is Co-Owner, Co-CEO of Streets2Schools (S2S). Through this venture, she directs a team of Victim's Advocates who works with violent offenders. The company is the first of its kind providing approved interactive virtually-based Anger Management and DV-BIP 52 Week Courses in California counties with expansion across the nation. S2S expands service to provide professional development courses to referring Corrections, Parole, and Probation officers. The battery of six courses serves to support, lead, and lift the officers working with offenders.

Denise is a highly-motivated and creative professional, dynamic and collaborative, an individual that welcomes fresh ideas, has initiative, and is dedicated and experienced in providing service to others. She offers more than forty years of experience in teaching, writing, consulting, facilitation, training, administration, child assessment, counseling, and psychology, complemented by a proven ability to motivate and add value to teams. She is a 2019 nominee for a JMT DNA Culture Award: Nurture Transformation.

Denise is known for her children's book, *Christopher's Anger* (WPS) and is the author of *Mending Broken Connections* (CRP).

You can connect with Denise at:

- denise.healy@streets2schools.com
- www.facebook.com/Denise Healy MA
- www.s2sdvonline.com

CHAPTER 3

FROM NO-WHERE TO NOW-HERE, BRINGING PRODUCTS TO MARKET

BY THEO PRODROMITIS

MY WHY

Did you ever have a pivot point in life and get turned in a direction that is extremely uncomfortable or uncertain? One of mine was when I was anticipating the birth of my first child. Prior to that, I enjoyed a successful career in the professional beauty industry, as a national sales trainer. All the luxuries I had enjoyed in my travels that included spa visits, would now take time and I just didn't have a lot of that. My mom and dad had passed away years ago; I missed their wisdom, and I needed advice on how to balance it all! Their amazing spirits resonated in my heart and mind. Thankfully, I had my incredible older sister Themie, with four children, to help guide me. I was determined to figure out how to include a little luxury in my new role and to launch a movement of self-care. My brother Dean, a beauty industry expert and I collaborated and came up with a plan. Our brand, Spa Destinations, was born.

THE LAUNCH

We decided to sell through an in-home party plan because it made sense to meet our target customers in the comfort and privacy of their homes. Not surprisingly, our budget was bigger than our personal funds, or small angel investors could handle. We found multimillion-dollar investors to serve in a key strategic, advisory role (and surrounded ourselves with incredible people). Our mission was now in motion!

BOOM

The journey was off to an amazing start. It was a combination of the hardest work I had ever done and the bliss of enjoying my new family. I was building a dream and legacy (no pressure). Life had another plan for us with the housing crisis/recession of 2008. Time to pivot again. This time I had three children under the age of five, was newly divorced, and everybody was hit hard financially. In-home parties declined, and unfortunately, so did our sales. We scaled back to the basic, most profitable products. Time to reinvent ourselves, stay true to the mission or go bankrupt. For the next several years, we held on tight. (We call those the white-knuckle years.)

EARLY ADOPTERS

E-commerce and the Amazon platform were gaining traction, but many of my colleagues feared Amazon. The magic of being able to reach customers 24/7 across the nation was quickly very clear. Having Amazon, an enormous logistics and marketing giant on our side (the 800-pound gorilla) was the spark that lit my fire again. I was invited to a Women's Entrepreneurship Conference. I was learning from an entirely new world of experts. While our growth has been exponential, we stay humble and flexible.

STAY RELEVANT

In 2018, we rebranded and relaunched our entire line of products, have been featured on TV, national publications, podcasts and more. I can't wait to share the biggest lessons we have learned.

A. Identify Why you want to launch
The most crucial question that needs to be answered before planning a product launch is …why? The top answers are (a) to make lots of money, (b) to help the world, (c) to leave your day job and (d) to share your genius and gain recognition.

Solution Products: These products solve unmet needs (usually of the inventor/ creator) and of course thousands (maybe hundreds of thousands) of others. This holy grail of products solves real problems that you are certain that others have. To come up with your own idea, simply walk through your house and make a list of every little thing that bothers you. Solution product ideas are born out of necessity. If it rains 70% of the time and your umbrella holder does not accommodate wet umbrellas dripping, a solution product is born. *This category has the highest percentage of patents.*

Passion Products: Do you just love a "work around" you came up with? A passion product is something you absolutely love and evangelize about without any compensation. Finally, it occurs to you (when other people keep saying, "wow, that is a great idea,") that it could be marketed. These are products that improve on an existing category that the creator knows well. For example, if a busy mom mixes her kid's yogurt, liquid vitamins and muffin together in a container because there is nothing that offers all three, she is creating a passion product. Passion products find you; you don't have to go looking for them. There is incredible potential here to build a brand known for ideas. *A trademarked name is critical to establish credibility.*

Private Label Products: In this day and age, you can get almost anything made for you to sell. The saying goes that "imitation is the greatest form of flattery." Are you creating something logical to complement your business? A yoga instructor can offer private label yoga pants and the finest yoga mats. Their clients already have a built-in need for the item, so tremendous value and convenience comes from the expertise in offering high quality. This product category has the lowest barrier to entry so you can focus most of your resources on marketing. The key is finding existing manufacturing in the USA or abroad, that can accommodate consistent quality and scaling quantity. *Don't be fooled if it appears too good to be true, do your research!*

THE TEST

Are you adding value for customers by creating it, combining it or making it available? Value can come from inventing it, creating it, sourcing it, putting it together or simply marketing it and bringing it to the attention of customers.

SUCCESS FORMULA TIP: Play the long game. Be certain that your financial needs and goals are in alignment. Most product launches will not produce an income for at least 18 months.

B. Money, Money, Money, Money

A crucial part of launching a product line is to figure out how you are going to pay for it. Many people are looking for a "get-rich-quick" plan, but they're missing some of the pieces of the story. Three ways to finance a project include:

#1. Your own money
#2. Friends and Family money
#3. Other people's money (crowd funding, angel investors, venture capital firms)

Most entrepreneurs start with #1 and grow into #2 and #3. Anything that can happen... and will happen during the research and development phase and bringing it to market. Be brutally honest with yourself. Do you have the grit, risk tolerance or desire to utilize other people's money? It's always going to cost more than you think. Finally, investing in quality is the single, most impactful action you can take.

Take a close look at your finances and budget what you can afford to invest. 100% funding may mean 100% control – however, you will be limited to what you know. Beware of falling in love with your idea because it can cloud your judgment or get you overextended. Once you have determined how much you will invest, the second option is family and friends who believe in your idea. You can often secure family and friends' investments with a conversation because they are investing in you (not just the product). Draft a simple agreement to ensure you have a mutual understanding that protects the relationship and the investment.

Demonstrate your professionalism, clarity of communication and understanding of business needs by developing an executive summary (one page or one sheet). Traditional investors, investment firms and venture capitalists will require it. This is a succinct overview and reference in an industry-standardized format. An executive summary includes:

- One-line product description
- Business Summary
- Management Team
- Customer Problem Solved
- Product
- Target Customers, Target Market
- Sales and Marketing Strategy
- Revenue Model (show me the money)
- Competitors
- Points of Difference (Competitive Advantage)

Watch episodes of "Shark Tank" where the very savvy, multimillion and billion-dollar investors ask the same questions over and over regardless of the product, service or category.

Do you have any intellectual property?

What are your current sales?

How much does it cost to make and how much do you sell it for?

Then they consider the entrepreneur's drive, upside potential and scalability. Key insights from the most successful entrepreneurs are revealed in this formula. Answer these questions for yourself as you go.

SUCCESS FORMULA TIPS: Track every dollar spent in research and development. Make formal agreements (even with friends and family) for all money invested. Consider hiring a fundraising professional when the time is right. You will be glad you did.

C. What is Intellectual Property Anyway?

An extremely important facet of launching a product is answering the question of intellectual property... is it protectable? One of my wisest investments has been working with amazing intellectual property lawyers. These key concepts will directly affect the success of your product launch journey. What is a trademark, a patent and a copyright?

Trademarks

A **trademark** is a word, phrase, symbol, and/or design that identifies and distinguishes the source of the goods of one party from those of others. (www.uspto.gov)

A **service mark** is a word, phrase, symbol, and/or design

that identifies and distinguishes the source of a service rather than goods. Some examples include: brand names, slogans, and logos. (www.uspto.gov)

A trademark can be either a word mark or design symbol or a combination of both, and these are registered with the United States Patent and Trademark Office (USPTO). There is an online application for up to $400 per product category. (automotive, beauty, etc.) Ensure accuracy and protection with your attorney, they know the nuances that will provide protection in the future. Don't cut corners on legal advice (or product quality).

Beware of scams/commercial sites or official-looking notices in the mail that attempt to interject themselves in the process but are not affiliated with the official agency. They often use government terms and Washington, DC addresses to confuse applicants. Third party website ownership can be researched at: www.whois.com. Use the official United States Patent and Trademark Office site: www.uspto.gov.

Patents
A property right granted by the Government of the United States of America to an inventor "to exclude others from making, using, offering for sale, or selling the invention throughout the United States or importing the invention into the United States" for a limited time in exchange for public disclosure of the invention when the patent is granted. (www.uspto.gov)

There are two different kinds of patents – utility patents and design patents. The patent process is intense, creative and requires incredible detail and resolve (and is far more expensive than a trademark). For products that are going to have a unique design feature, it will be critical to begin the patent process and to do the research on existing products in that category. You will need a technical drawing or engineering rendering before applying. Avoid marketing scams that target "inventors" by promising to make it easy and cheap. Intellectual Property Attorneys will advise you on accomplishing your goals with either United States (www. uspto.gov) or the World Intellectual Property Organization (www.wipo.int).

Copyrights

(a) Copyright protection subsists, in accordance with this title, in original works of authorship fixed in any tangible medium of expression, now known or later developed, from which they can be perceived, reproduced, or otherwise communicated, either directly or with the aid of a machine or device. – United States Copyright Office (USCO), online at www.copyright.gov.

Copyrights can extend to literary, musical, dramatic works, pictorial, motion pictures, sound recording, architectural works. They do not protect ideas, procedures, processes, systems, methods of operation, concepts, principles or discoveries.

Do You Use Independent Contractors?

Please consider some sage advice about hiring independent contractors to do creative work for your company, like website developers, graphic artists, photographers, ad copy writers, researchers, etc. Although state laws vary, a general rule is that independent contractors will own the work product that they create for you – not you. You will need them to sign a written assignment to you (or your company) to ensure ownership. Work done by employees as part of their job duties, on the other hand, is generally owned by the company. Best practices include having all employees sign a written assignment when they create valuable work for your company.

Liability

In addition to registering trademarks, patents and copyrights, it is equally important to avoid infringing on the intellectual property of others. This is crucial because "ignorance is no defense" under the law (although knowingly infringing can lead to enhanced damages against you in court). Imagine launching a big ad campaign only to get a "cease and desist" demanding that you change your trademark. "Corporate shield" protection that comes with incorporating may not protect you. Liability for these types of claims is personal, meaning you could be on the hook personally for damages even if your company cannot pay.

SUCCESS FORMULA TIPS: Understand Trademarks, Patents and Copyrights (having them doesn't guarantee that your product will sell). Always consult your IP Attorney.

D. Manufacturing

There are benefits of physically making the product yourself in the beginning. Iron out the kinks before seeking any type of patent or trademark protection. Gather market feedback and make revisions for maximum efficiency. For manufacturers, the key questions to ask include; set up fees, minimum quantities, volume discounts and lead times. Private label products can be made in the U.S. or abroad and most times are not considered for patents because they are not proprietary.

Thomasnet (www.thomasnet.com) can help steer you to U.S. manufacturing depending on the materials utilized, high-tech or low-tech components and intellectual property. When you are physically making a product, you will be responsible for the ingredients/ components and performance with increased liability. Manufacturers will carry their own liability insurance to help mitigate the risk. The truth is that many other countries do not recognize or respect trademarks and patents when manufacturing and it is expensive to seek remedies for infringements.

Manufacturing Pros and Cons

U.S. Manufacturing	International Manufacturing
Governed by US laws & USPTO	Manufacturing is not and subject to US Trademark and Patent law but sales in the US are.*
Higher Cost (generally)	Lower Cost
Quality Control	Low to No control over quality without direct representation in that country.
Shorter Turnaround time	Subject to longer lead times, higher cost to expedite orders internationally, political changes and tariffs.
	* It is an infringement to make, use, sell, or offer to sell a product in the US that is the subject of a US patent. Ignorance is no defense – you can be liable even if you don't know about the patent.

Research whether international counterfeit/knock offs are an issue in your industry.

SUCCESS FORMULA TIPS: Production quality, availability and volume capacity can make or break your product. Quality builds sustainable brands.

BRAND PROMISE

Your product can help bring a brand to life but is not "the brand." Core values, practices, integrity, customer experiences and impressions create the feeling and story of a brand. A brand lives in a sacred place in the hearts and minds of consumers and drives engagement and purchasing behavior.

Thank you for taking this journey with me.

Time to Light Your Fire. Opa!

About Theo

Theo's lifelong passion for business is born of "philotimo," a distinctly Greek personal and cultural imperative that life has a deeper meaning through larger contributions; to honor your God-given gifts by improving the lives of others.

Theo Prodromitis learned business values, ethics and tenacity at an early age from her vivacious, business-savvy, Greek family. She ran her first retail venture at age 8, naturally thriving amid the personal connections, science and craft of her entrepreneurial success.

Through decades of visionary executive leadership as a CEO, successful Amazon entrepreneur and expert marketing strategist, she creates exponential growth and profits for her own companies and hundreds of others. Theo's expertise spans business development and intellectual property, manufacturing and logistics, and to marketing and strategic communications. She is a sought-after spokesperson and fierce advocate for the interests of women in business and small businesses nationwide.

Under her leadership as co-founder and CEO of Spa Destinations, the company became an early adopter of the emerging Amazon Marketplace platform, rocketing its post-recession growth trajectory. Theo was selected for the Amazon Women's Entrepreneur Conference and spoke at Amazon's BOOST Conference.

Theo Prodromitis became an Amazon Business Advocate, as well as taking on a leadership and advocacy role in support of favorable national policies for small businesses. In that capacity, she led the Amazon Business Advocate Delegate meeting with seven Congressional leaders on the Small Business Committee. She was nominated by Amazon and won a 2018 National Retail Federation "Champions of Retail" Award. As an honoree, Theo lobbied Congressional leaders on behalf of the 42 million Americans in retail and serves on the NRF Small Business Retail Advisory Council.

As Founder and CEO of Out Front Brands, Theo consults in branding, product development, sustainability and fast-growth businesses. Clients develop unique brand DNA, align marketing communications, discover opportunities for corporate evolution, and implement creative e-commerce strategies.

Theo Prodromitis is an award-winning trainer and national speaker. She has been a guest speaker at Amazon Headquarters, Seattle, WA, Voice America, Working Women of Tampa Bay, University of South Florida, St. Petersburg's Entrepreneurship Program, National Retail Federation podcast, a productivity trainer for Fortune 500 companies, and a presenter at The Home Depot Innovation Center. She was a Cultural Sensitivity Training Specialist for The International Indian Film Academy (IIFA) Awards, Visit Tampa Bay and Downtown Tampa Partnership Guest Experience Training.

She has been featured in the *National Retail Federation Retail Gets Real, Small Business Journal* on International Women's Day, *Business News Daily, Tampa Bay Times* and *Small Biz Daily.* Features include: Amazon Blog, Day One, Stories of Entrepreneurship, Storefront Women-Owned Business feature and Storefront of the Week, Yahoo Finance, Bay News 9, ABC Action News, FOX 13 and NBC.

Theo champions many philanthropic causes, including women and children's health and safety and sustainability. She holds a Political Science degree from the University of South Florida and Yale University Certificate in The Science of Well Being.

Theo is the dedicated mother of Mary, Jacqueline and Spero as well as the organizer of her big Greek family reunions.

CHAPTER 4

YOU ARE LOVE

BY VICTORIA LOWERY

The power of awareness: feel confident, attract love,
live a joyous life, and heal the world

Once upon a time, there was a beautiful girl who met a handsome prince…and they lived happily ever after. Wait a minute! Insert screeching sound! Stop right here! So all they had to do was meet, gaze into each other's eyes, maybe climb a tower or ride a horse and feel that "magic"? If that's all there is to it, then why does happily-ever-after end in divorce for 50% of all marriages? And why do nearly 50% of Americans feel lonely, left out, isolated, lack companionship and their relationships lack meaning, according to the most recent U.S. Loneliness Index?[1]

As a child, I had my own oversized, elaborately-illustrated books containing fairy tales by Hans Christian Anderson and other great writers. I loved these beautiful books. While I knew they were fantasy, I, and surely many others, have longed for some modern-day version of them to be my reality. I'm here to tell you it can be. It starts with loving yourself, which allows your true self to emerge, and turns you into a love magnet, living a joyous life.

---

1. https://www.usnews.com/news/health-care-news/articles/2018-05-01/
   study-many-americans-report-feeling-lonely-younger-generations-more-so

How do I know, you ask?

I didn't. Like for years. Maybe even decades. Well past when I needed to know to make life-altering decisions.

I first met the one I thought was my soulmate, and foolishly squandered that. Then, I married someone I didn't really know, even though we dated for six years first. That ended in the divorce I thought I'd never have, and me learning a whole lot about the word sociopath.

But I'm a good person. I'm intelligent, motivated, performed well in school, had a college scholarship to play tennis after having been the only female athlete on the men's team at my first college. I'm reasonably attractive, a good listener, affectionate, and most people say I'm very kind. So, "what's wrong with me?"

Whether it's a friend, family member, date, co-worker or life partner, this is the inevitable question we ask ourselves when a relationship is rocky or doesn't last. On the surface, we can be experts at blaming the other person. But subconsciously, doubt gets buried like a little seed planted in the brain. This self-esteem stomping seed grows, wreaking havoc with your future. And it's entirely unnecessary.

The green couch and a flash of knowing

So there I was, sitting on our green couch, raising three daughters by myself, and wondering how someone so well-intentioned could go so wrong. I wasn't stupid, and my parents set an example of staying together. Then it struck me that the odds of getting either outcome, heads or tails, in a coin toss are 50%. Huh, a coin toss has the exact same odds of a marriage lasting? There had to be something I didn't know. There had to be some way everybody could increase their odds over that of a random coin toss. Then, like a bolt of lightning, the *Yes Test* appeared in my head. I quickly wrote it down. Right away I felt this was meant for more than just me. But how was I qualified to share such wisdom? So it sat out-of-site, but not out-of-mind, in my laptop for a year. It beckoned me until the growing passion in my soul could not be ignored.

So I put myself on a speaking tour going to every Rotary meeting, Kiwanis club, school, radio station, TV station or organization that was willing to listen, and usually offered a free lunch. I passed out surveys, gauged reactions, and actively applied the feedback. I researched, read books and wrote. I'd always been a deep-thinker and compassionate listener and found that I could be helpful as a life coach. I became known as a 'relationship expert' and started my own radio show. Interestingly, after receiving an education in marketing and finance, and a career as CEO of a large organization, people were calling me "The Love Lady." Life's unexpected journey is so incredible.

We were smart in Kindergarten

One of my favorite book titles is, *All I Really Need to Know I Learned in Kindergarten*. Life's foundation was laid then and knowing what to do was simple:

> Share; don't hit; play fair; tell the truth; say sorry when you've hurt someone; put things back where you found them; hold hands and stick together; clean up your own mess; don't take what's not yours; eat healthy snacks and wash your hands first; play with whatever toys you want as long as you don't break them, hurt yourself or others; and The Golden Rule, treat others like you want to be treated.

There you have it. It's really not complicated. If we stopped right here and applied these as adults, we'd be in darn good shape.

So why does life get complicated? The answer is a mindset of intentional remembering.

I learned as CEO that great business plans just sit on the shelf as really expensive paper if there's no action plan to go with it. A plan must be checked at every meeting, tasks assigned, and adjustments made for the business to stay on course. In terms of life, we already know the essentials really. What we need to become aware of is that inner joy requires daily attention. Like staying physically fit requires regular visits to the gym, so too must we regularly attend the emotional gym. It only takes a day, one tv show, one hurtful comment, one look at a magazine, one failed-attempt, one comparison, mistake, loss, or doubt, for what we learned in kindergarten to get fuzzy.

Going to the emotional gym includes reading or listening to books, working regularly with a coach, counselor or mentor; praying, meditating, and meeting in groups; journaling and being open with a trusted friend; connecting with nature and feeling unconditional love especially from children or pets; taking classes or calling mom. Do any of this and more daily. Stay connected. Take action to remember and continually grow.

Self-love first

You've likely heard the saying, "To love someone else, you must first love yourself." I whole-heartedly agree. In fact, most problems in relationships can be traced to some dissatisfaction with self. Life is one big mirror. We launch ourselves out to experience the world, our disappointments, doubts and fears cleverly hidden behind the glass, but the world sees clearly. The energy of truth cannot be blocked from eventually reflecting back.

Three things I want you to know:

1. Owning your truth is essential.
   I ask myself, "How in a world full of photo filters and competition can I express the magnificence of you with all your perceived imperfections?" For the answer, I went to my spiritual gym of meditation to hear, "that's the way

God made me." This is not a commentary on religion but an acknowledgment that we all came from a divine source.

Add to this what our culture considers beautiful changes over time. During the Renaissance Period (1400s thru the 1600s) for example, great artists painted women as full-figured because this was considered most desirable. If you are full-figured today, you must be a 'renaissance being'! It's fashion that has changed, not truth.

The Golden Rule is one of those we learned in kindergarten. If someone makes a hurtful full-figure comment, they have forgotten the rule. They are not coming from a place of love. Only you can choose to take it in as painful. If you love your body, you will not identify with the joke. Besides, someday it may cause you to meet the love of your life at The Society for Renaissance Figures meeting. You just never know.

2. <u>Your path is noble.</u>
   Your life is your gift to the world. Some are meant to go to college, while some have no education and start a successful business in their garage. Some are great athletes, while others have two left feet but sing like a canary. Some will give birth to twelve children while others have no children but run a shelter for lost animals. These are different ways of using your talents to give to the world. Every bit of it matters. Equally! Loved ones may have well-intentioned advice. Aunt Mary might say you need to be an astronaut ("the benefits are great, and you get to travel"), when nothing makes you happier than a paintbrush in your hand. No apologies need be made for choosing the path that inspires you. "I love you Aunt Mary and will invite you to my first art show. Pass the peas, please."

And no good will come from comparing your unique path to anyone else's unique path. You could be feeling great about the used Hyundai you worked and saved three years for, and then see someone else's shiny Mustang and suddenly lose your joy. Maybe the Mustang owner lost their home and is living in their car. You never know what learning you are in need of, what the next horizon is, or why each of you is where you are. Simply trust the process, pay attention, and enjoy.

3. <u>You are not alone.</u>
The second you think nobody else feels like you do, think again. If you've ever felt isolated, emotional, defeated, different, or felt you had to conform to fit in, rejoice, because you are in abundant company. When this happens, simply go back to the emotional gym. Most likely there is some nice growth coming your way. You are worth the lesson.

Finding gratitude and doing kind things for others are also great pick-me-ups.

Awareness is more

We've all heard the phrase, "knowledge is power." Let's give the word knowledge a bigger reach by adding the idea of awareness to it. To me, awareness is not only knowing the facts, but it's also a heightened state of observation. It's being in tune with yourself and staying present in the moment.

There are some simple but critical elements to be aware of in those three little dots (i.e., …) before the 'happily ever after'. The nine questions, born on the green couch, that I'm about to give you, go a long way to fill that gap. They will empower you to make relationship decisions you feel good about. It's important because the person you choose as a life partner will have dramatic influence over every area of your life.

Circle Yes or No

The *Yes Test* is nine questions answered with a yes or no. (We like to keep things simple around here.) All yes answers mean you have a green light for 'go' in the relationship. Any no answer is a major red flag.

1) Do you know and can you support his/her goals and dreams? *Yes* *No*
2) Would you still love him/her if the way he/she looks changes for the worse? *Yes* *No*
3) Does he/she welcome your opinion? *Yes* *No*
4) Do you like who you are when you're together? *Yes* *No*
5) Do you trust him/her? *Yes* *No*
6) Do you both want a lifetime commitment at the same time? *Yes* *No*
7) Do you both either want or not want children? *Yes* *No*
8) We are in agreement on how we will make financial decisions? *Yes* *No*
9) Can you be monogamous as mutually agreed? *Yes* *No*

Following the *Yes Test* are factors that aren't deal breakers, but do require pre-emptive agreement. It's appropriately called, The Agreement List. It includes religious differences, friends and family, shared activities and common values.

The *Yes Test* is helpful to married, committed or engaged couples by identifying areas of struggle. But ideally, we are all given the opportunity to learn before investing in lifetime decisions.

The capacity to feel romantic love develops in our teen years. Six couples in my high school class alone of only 86 students, dated and eventually married. That's a total of 14%!

There are too many who have taken their own life or suffered in destructive marriages or friendships. Too many have lost careers and companies set-back because of internal relationship conflicts. Government is feeling the pressure to legislate human personality. The answer is not more laws, but more education –

the gift of emotional equipment – allowing the brightest and best qualities in every human to shine.

We have the ability to shape our world, by empowering each individual with more awareness.

About Victoria

Observing the great impact relationships have on both personal and professional success, Victoria Lowery left her career as a CEO to become an advocate for social and emotional education.

Victoria was born and raised in the Midwest where baseball and apple pie set the tone. Where faith, family, and farming are the three pillars of life. Her own dad would have been a priest if it weren't for his desire for family and having a farm. Victoria was raised with "marriage is forever" and if that marriage isn't working, that's "your cross to bear." Despite this, she found the courage to leave her own unfixable marriage.

Professionally, Victoria started working at age 15 as a model and did book-keeping for an investment company. At age 22, her first endeavor into rescuing a business was the family-owned supper club she renovated, operated, then sold.

She became Mrs. Ohio 2001. One of the local TV stations that interviewed her as Mrs. Ohio, soon offered her a position as talk show host. After several successful seasons here, the aftermath of 9-11 led to a critical fork in the road. Many non-profit events were canceled, and advertising dollars were tight. So Victoria accepted the CEO position at the local Chamber of Commerce. Eventually she became CEO of Ohio's professional association of Chamber executives, strategically based within walking distance from the state capital building.

In all of these fantastic professional experiences, Victoria saw the root solution to virtually every business or political issue that arose, as solvable when non-ego-based enlightened minds were involved. *This is where the real difference is made*, she thought.

Victoria also recognized that greater awareness at an earlier age would have dramatically affected the choices in her own personal life. Life's toughest lessons are where the brightest light shines through. She believes that a *grass-roots-type effort providing emotional learning at an earlier age must take place.*

Fueled by her professional and personal observations and experiences, Victoria became an award-winning author, life coach and speaker. She is driven to see a reduced divorce rate, less stress, and more joy for everyone.

CHAPTER 5

LEVEL UP FOR SUCCESS BY TRANSFORMING STRESS

BY WENDY A. WARD, MD

Over the years, I started to recognize the rapid increase of a disturbing pattern emerging for countless people on their quest-for-success journeys. "Success *keys, tools and formulas*" or *Dream Builders*, were being undermined at an alarming and detrimental rate, especially for the younger generations. There was a *Predator* hiding in plain sight that was *destroying* the *pursuit and maintenance* of Success and Dreams, as well as *taking lives.* That Predator is Chronic Stress.

Most people aren't aware that Chronic Stress has been declared a Public Health Crisis for both Youth and Adults. It's not only a *deadly* predator but also a very *sneaky* predator which is why it's so dangerous. Subconsciously, we accept the daily stressors we encounter in our lives as normal. As a result, we don't even realize we're in the relentless grip of Chronic Stress being thrown into Survival Mode, until it's too late.

When Chronic Stress catapults you into Survival Mode, you can't focus, concentrate, make decisions, be creative, problem-solve, sleep right, eat right, and you lose joy and happiness. Simply put, you go completely haywire mentally, emotionally and physically. Due to the fact that Chronic Stress produces biochemical changes in the brain and body, you can't just "Snap out of it" or "Get over it."

It was 2016 when I had my experience with the *Predator*, in a situation that lasted over two years. My job at that time where I'd been employed as an Anesthesiologist for twenty years had reorganized, eliminating my position. My Mom, my best friend, became gravely ill with multi-systemic disease. The emotional toll of watching my Mom suffer requiring numerous hospitalizations and my role as caretaker was overwhelming. Superimposed on this already challenging situation, my Dad was in and out of the hospital with recurrent bouts of Pneumonia, my younger sister suffered a nearly-fatal bleeding brain aneurysm and spent almost a year between the hospital and a rehabilitation facility, and my Dad's wife passed away. I was spent mentally, emotionally and physically, trying to manage all of these situations effectively. The five hours a day commuting between three different hospitals across two states didn't make things any easier. Before my Mom, Dad or Sister had a chance to recover, my Mom passed away. I was devastated. Survival Mode was in full effect.

What's interesting was that I was experiencing exactly what I'd been witnessing for countless others on their *'quest for success'* journeys. You see, prior to these overwhelming events in 2016, my spirit prompted me to start my company **MPower Productions** which would provide a *consistent* platform for my *calling* and purpose, doing work as a Life Transformation Specialist. While I love medicine, I'm a Renaissance woman gifted with a variety of 'gifts, talents and abilities' that range from being a healer, motivator and educator to singer/songwriter, filmmaker, and athlete. **MPower** allows me to utilize all of my Talents to empower both Youth and Adults to Survive, Thrive and Succeed so they can live happy productive and gratifying lives of purpose. *This is my passion and dream!*

Although I'd been doing **MPower**-related work occasionally, my *soul* had been pulling me in the direction of committing to **MPower** full time for a while. I believe that this shift at my job was a divine push and confirmation that the time had come to let go of the 'sure' and pursue my *calling* full time. Understandably, I had mixed emotions. I was super excited about pursuing my passion which allowed me to embrace and express my creative side fully. However, I was also profoundly anxious about leaving the predictability and financial security of my thirty-year comfort zone as a Physician and heading out into the foreign and uncharted waters of the business world *full time* as a *first-time* Entrepreneur.

The timing of my situation couldn't be more ironic. I taught 'Stress Management and Success Training' to help others combat the *Predator* on their success journeys. Now, just as I was starting out trying to gain momentum on *my* new success journey to build **MPower**, the Predator struck thrusting me into Survival Mode. I was unable to fully engage or be effective with any of my efforts regarding business endeavors.

It's no surprise that Chronic Stress is definitely an inevitable *equal opportunist* that doesn't discriminate when it comes to wreaking havoc on your life and sabotaging *success plans*. Recognizing its presence is the *first* step to managing it and optimism is always beneficial. It's been quoted that "Adversity causes some to break and others to *break records*." My hope has always been to *transform* and *break records* in the *midst* of adversity. This inspired me to create an easy-to-follow *STRESS MANAGEMENT TRANSFORMATION TOOL* called the **MPower 'STRESS-BUSTER FORMULA'** which can help empower anyone to *consistently break records* in the *midst* of adversity. It's what empowered me to effectively *transform stress* and *Level Up* to resume my success journey.

Unquestionably, having an effective STRESS MANAGEMENT PLAN (which *includes* Transformation Tools, Counseling with a Medical Professional and Suicide Prevention Hotline Contact Information) as the foundation for *every* TOTAL LIFE SUCCESS PLAN, is *essential* for personal 'safety and well-being' *and* preserving, fortifying, upgrading and optimally executing that SUCCESS PLAN.

IMPORTANT: For *LIFE-THREATENING STRESS, CONSULT A MEDICAL PROFESSIONAL <u>IMMEDIATELY</u> &/or CONTACT THE SUICIDE PREVENTION HOTLINE.*

The **MPower '*STRESS-BUSTER* FORMULA'**

The **MPower '*STRESS-BUSTER* FORMULA'** is a simple, easy-to-remember *6-STEP STRESS MANAGEMENT TRANSFORMATION TOOL* that conveniently utilizes the acronym **S.T.R.E.S.S.** to outline its steps.

It meets stress head-on, providing *first steps* strategically designed to accomplish the following:

1. *Immediately stop* – the *destructive* Stress Response.
2. Show you *how to shift gears* – from *Survival Mode to Thrival Mode.*
3. *Transform Stress* – empowering you to *Level Up* for S*uccess and Happiness.*

That's **S.T.R.E.S.S.**

S = STOP!!!

Sit down or lie down. When you *physically* STOP, it allows you to *consciously* calm yourself and the CHAOS in your Mind, Spirit and Emotions…and CENTER yourself. It keeps you from continuing to *move mindlessly*, trying to do everything at once, accomplishing nothing – which *increases* stress.

T = TAKE '3 DEEP BREATHS'

Take '3 Deep Breaths'... *specifically* – ABDOMINAL or DIAPHRAGMATIC deep breaths – where you take a long, slow, deep breath *IN* – so that *only* your belly pushes out while your chest doesn't rise - and then breathe *OUT.* Pause for a moment after each breath and repeat. This is your scientifically proven *BUILT-IN STRESS RELIEVER* that calms your body, mind, and emotions.

The great thing is, you already know how to do it! Deep breathing activates the body's natural ability to relax via biochemical mechanisms. It relaxes and calms the chaotic physical, mental and emotional responses to stress. Also, focusing on your breathing distracts you from focusing on your problems, additionally creating a state of relaxation and calm.

Taking *DIAPHRAGMATIC BREATHS,* which is the basis for most MEDITATION techniques, can *prevent and reduce* stress and anxiety when done for approximately 20 – 30 minutes per day.

R = REMEMBER

Think back on a stressful, challenging trial from your past...a situation you thought you'd never get through and thought would never end, but it's over now. Most trials are temporary.

It's been said, "Nothing good lasts forever." The good news is, "Nothing bad lasts *forever*" either. Some trials last long and strong. You've gotten through them before and you will again.

Next, REMEMBER that trial with even greater depth, clarity and introspection. You'll see that you didn't just *go* through the experience, you also managed to *grow* through the experience, learning, acquiring and/or strengthening something valuable and empowering, along the way!

This truth lies in the equation:

TRIALS + TRANSFORMATION = TRIUMPH
TRIALS inspire... *Level Up* **TRANSFORMATION**...
that *equips* you to **TRIUMPH!!!**

I'm a firm believer that everything happens for a reason; no trial is a waste unless you *don't* learn something; trials happen *for* you not *to* you...*activating your greatness within*...preparing you to achieve and maintain the success you desire; and trials provide *lessons for blessings*.

When I took stock of my situation, *patience, the value of slowing down, living a balanced life* and maintaining a *consistent 'attitude of gratitude and present moment awareness'* are a few valuable lessons and tools that were strengthened or acquired by me. These qualities are imperative for my life in general, and success with **MPower**. Additionally, this experience *blessed* me because it allowed me to spend *extra* quality time with my Mom before she passed.

E = ELEVATE YOUR PERSPECTIVE

Elevate Your Perspective ...so you can *rise above* the Trial and view it from a *higher clearer* perspective. This is the most *important powerful thought-shifting Level Up transformation step* in the **MPower 'STRESS-BUSTER Formula'**.

PERSPECTIVE is *everything*. It allows you to control *how* any trial affects you. The mere *presence* of a trial *doesn't* induce stress or catapult you into Survival Mode. The *'reality, degree of Stress and magnitude'* of Survival Mode disturbances *experienced*, is *solely determined* by your *perception* about the trial. PERSPECTIVE dictates how you think, feel and ultimately respond to a trial. Coach John Wooden said: "If you change the way you look at things, the way things look will change."

I remember watching a news report about the California Wildfires. The Reporter interviewed two couples, side by side, in front of the rubble and ashes where their homes once stood. Couple #1 was understandably, visibly devastated and in tears. When asked how they felt, they responded *that they had lost everything and didn't know how they were ever going to recover.*

Astonishingly, Couple #2 felt *blessed and were thankful to GOD 'they lost no one, what was lost could be replaced' and that this was a great opportunity for them to start over.* Same degree of loss, two totally different *PERSPECTIVES.*

Optimistic PERSPECTIVES allow you to learn, grow and *Level Up* your wisdom and life tools; focus on solutions not problems; see blessings in the lessons; and experience healthier quicker returns to restoration on all levels. PERSPECTIVE is *key* in hastening your *shift* from Survival Mode to Thrival Mode and on to Success!

S = SILLY

Activate your Inner Child! SILLY is a fun step you can do anytime, anywhere, any place that immediately *knocks out* the *Stress Beast.* There's *truth* in the quote, "Laughter is the best medicine." In fact, it's been *scientifically proven* that being silly or anything that makes you laugh, have fun, enjoy yourself or feel good like 'humor, jokes, exercise, playing games, hobbies, entertainment, music, singing, dancing, etc.' – release 'feel good hormones' that literally *enhance* your overall sense of *well-being.*

SCIENTIFIC FACT: It's IMPOSSIBLE to FEEL WORRY *while* you're FEELING GOOD!

S = STRATEGIZE…with SERENITY

This *mega-empowering* step allows you to *complete the process to LEVEL UP FOR SUCCESS BY TRANSFORMING STRESS!!!*

STRATEGIZE

Learn, grow and use your *newly acquired Level Up 'wisdom and life tools'* to do the following:

1. Reflect on the trial(s) and make a list of the lessons you've learned and qualities that were strengthened or acquired.
2. Use your *Level Up* wisdom to create, fortify or upgrade your Success Plan
3. *Believe* your dreams are possible and visualize it in what I call *Real-D* as if it's already done.
4. Take massive *it's impossible to fail* action steps, doing everything within your power, ability and control to carry out your plan with flexibility, focusing on taking *only* the *next best step*, moving forward *one step at a time.*

Then...

with SERENITY: Surrender! Relax, let go and let GOD, the Divine, the Universe or whatever your belief system is, do the rest.

Embrace the principles in:

THE SERENITY PRAYER
I ACCEPT the things I cannot change,
have COURAGE to change the things I can,
and the WISDOM to know the difference.

Finally, relax, choose happiness and enjoy life! We can't control the *trials that appear* in our lives, but we *do* have *full control* over our responses, choices and decisions we make during them.

REMEMBER:
(a) TRIALS are inevitable.
(b) TRANSFORMATION is under your control.
(c) TRIUMPH is yours for the taking.

The MPower *'STRESS-BUSTER FORMULA'* empowers you to *LEVEL UP FOR SUCCESS BY TRANSFORMING STRESS!!!*

About Dr. Wendy

Dr. Wendy A. Ward helps her clients transform their way of 'thinking, being, doing and behaving', empowering them to survive, thrive and succeed.

Wendy is a Physician – a Board Certified Anesthesiologist who has been practicing medicine for 30 years – and a Life Transformation Specialist. She received her Bachelor of Science degree in Microbiology from the University of Massachusetts-Amherst and her Medical Degree from Mount Sinai School of Medicine in New York City. Wendy is also certified in the holistic disciplines of Acupuncture and Reflexology.

Wendy, a true Renaissance woman, is the founder and CEO of **MPower Productions** – a multimedia inspirational educational company – which she started ten years ago. **MPower** allows her to feed her passion and use her eclectic array of talents and expertise, which include being a Healer, Educator, Singer/Songwriter, Storyteller, Filmmaker, Inspirational Speaker, Author and Athlete, to serve. As the daughter of an Educator and a Physician, her inherent passion and aptitude to 'heal, inspire, educate, uplift and empower' others, especially Youth, is woven into her DNA.

Wendy's philosophy is that everyone has a purpose and deserves an even playing field of opportunity to maximize their full potential, realize their dreams and fulfill that purpose. She believes that as each person is able to fulfill their purpose, collectively, it serves as a major precursor to achieving the ultimate goal of establishing world 'love, peace and unity', creating a win-win for all.

Dr. Ward created the *CPR (Continuous Positive Reinforcement) for eMPOWERment* multimedia content platform to implement her empowerment efforts. This platform includes her signature *MPOWER 'STRESS MANAGEMENT & SUCCESS' TRAINING SYSTEM*, which is designed to empower her clients to *survive* any life challenge, *thrive* in the face of adversity and *succeed* in every aspect of their lives. Teamwork and her 'scientific and spiritually-based' *reach to teach approach* are the cornerstones of this system. She employs the utilization of multimedia interactive Youth-friendly vehicles that include Music, Audio-Visual Entertainment (Films, Shows, Gaming, etc.), Sports and

Social Media. This enables her to *'reach'* youth by meeting them in their familiar 'comfort and passion' zone, allowing her to effectively *'teach'* and empower them.

Wendy embodies her philosophy and beliefs not only through her work with **MPower**, but also by partnering and participating for over 35 years with various Charitable, Educational and Youth Empowerment organizations. She contributes her time, talent and resources as a mentor, participant and/ or co-creator in countless empowering 'events, forums and platforms' for both Youth and Adults. Some of the organizations Wendy participates with include The Rotary, New York City Department of Education, New Jersey Department of Education, New York Foundling Preventive Program and countless other charitable and educational organizations and endeavors.

While Wendy's primary focus is the empowerment of adolescent youth, her utilization of an 'intergenerational – it takes a village' model for youth empowerment, allows her to 'train, teach and empower' adults to survive, thrive and succeed as well, which empowers communities.

You can connect with Wendy at:

- wendyward@mpowerproductions.com
- www.facebook.com/wendy.a.ward1

CHAPTER 6

YOUR SIDE OF THE TABLE

BY AARON R. SMITH, M.B.A

MY SIDE OF THE TABLE

In my early years of work in commercial construction, there was a specific moment during my first major project that led to the creation of a phrase I have used regularly since. I was new to the industry but, nevertheless, found myself sitting in a conference room during a contentious high-level discussion between school officials, an architect, and a contractor (for whom I worked). A major problem had come up on a school construction project, and each party was digging in on their side of the issue. It was a classic "whose-fault-is-this?" scenario. I was young and not terribly involved in the actual issue over which they were fighting, so many things flew right over my head as the conversation intensified. When the meeting was over, I went to my car and called my brother who is an attorney. I explained the meeting to him and asked for his thoughts. He then asked me, "Were there any lawyers there?" I told him that yes, the school's attorney was sitting with the school officials. He then told me, "You really should not be in a meeting like that without an attorney on your side of the table, too."

"My side of the table." The phrase stuck with me, and I have used it as a quick guide to evaluate everything since, from my potential effectiveness in a contentious board room to my likelihood for success on a project. In my line of work, figuring out who is on my side of the table may be as simple as asking, "Who are the subcontractors on this project?" or "Do I have an expert in local building codes going into this meeting with me?" For you it is likely something else. But the people on your side of the table *will* determine your success. I have found this to be true in both construction projects and in business. The key to success is packing your side of the table with people who cover your blind spots and fight for your best interests.

In this chapter, I will use construction projects as the narrative through which I will explain the need to have the right people on your side of the table – but this concept is not unique to my industry. An evaluation of the team working for your best interests is vital to success in all industries.

DEALING WITH UNKNOWNS!

If you have ever managed a construction project of any size, you have probably come close to losing your mind. That is true even for those of us who are professionals in the field of construction services. Building projects are notorious for their likelihood to have unforeseen conditions that lead to increased costs, material availability shortages, design flaws, and a myriad of other landmines just waiting to reveal themselves. And to compound these stressful elements of construction, the problems often require high-dollar fixes. The pressure is high, and the difficulties are many.

The old saying "if it was easy, everyone would do it" is especially true regarding building construction. Many people do not want the headaches and often razor-thin margins that accompany this line of work. So, understandably, they move on to other fields that better suit their skill set or interests. Unfortunately, however, at some point in their careers most high-level leaders find themselves knee-deep in a project that stretches them past their level of comfort and training. The example below is a common picture of how we can find ourselves far outside our proverbial "wheelhouse." If you look closely, you may see yourself in it.

NOT WHAT I SIGNED UP FOR

My father was a high school band director. Upon seeing *The Sound of Music* on a class trip, he knew that music would be the passion of his life. They say, "do what you love, and you will never work a day in your life," so he enjoyed every moment of fulfilling his passion. Then, a funny thing happened. He got married and had children. Flash forward a few years and he was a high school principal. Flash forward a few more and he was the superintendent of a school district. Before he knew it, this 60s-music-loving education enthusiast was managing four principals, 50+ teachers, 100+ support staff, K-12 curriculum, and a multi-million-dollar budget for his school. It was everything he had worked for.

Then, one day, state funding allowed his district to build a new elementary school. Overnight, in addition to his *actual* job, he found himself tasked with overseeing a multi-million-dollar construction project on behalf of the school district. After years of training and experience that allowed him to successfully evaluate and implement state and federal education initiatives, he now found himself making decisions on change orders for bad soil conditions, asbestos abatement, and a litany of other construction-related items for which he had no training. That was not what he signed up for.

Sadly, many of us find ourselves in similar situations. We are all different: public-school administrators, entrepreneurs with growing businesses, the leader of a growing branch of a company, or city and county officials, but we all find ourselves in the same unfortunate position. We are all diving into the deep end of building construction with nothing to go on except, at best, the advice of an architect who we know will mislead us to cover their tracks if problems arise.

HIRE A "BOB"

As we encounter these difficult positions in our roles as leaders, we are forced to make key decisions as to who will be on our team for large projects. Projects that are outside of the responsibilities we were trained to handle. There are two key "types" of people I am always adamant to have on my side of the table: a "Bob" and a "Sage."

In my company, we refer to an expert on a key issue who is brought in from the outside as a "Bob." The term is proudly pulled from the 1999 comedy "Office Space" wherein two outside consultants, both named Bob, come into the fictional technology firm of "Initech" to help with their corporate downsizing. We invite Bobs in when we have a project or problem that lands outside of our normal work competencies. The idea is that we do not pretend that we are experts in areas where we are not (and, more importantly, where others are).

For example, recently a local bank in my city merged with another local bank one city over. The result was a good-sized regional bank. The idea that the sitting presidents of each bank could have simply added to their skillsets the time and expertise required to oversee a bank merger is nothing short of ludicrous. As a board member of that bank, you would want to make sure you brought in a Bob. The benefit is two-fold. The Bob brings expertise to your specific project as well as keeps your existing personnel from becoming poor performers in their normal responsibilities by not over-taxing them.

Another good example from my own experience comes from a multi-year, multi-phase, multi-million-dollar construction project for a high school. The total project was north of 65 million dollars in cost, and it was spread over ten separate construction projects and five years. When the project started, the school superintendent was already dedicating well over 40 hours a week to the business of running a school district. The facilities director barely had enough time in his week to maintain the eight buildings under his supervision. The school board president was the owner and CEO of a large business in the region. *Even with the best of intentions,* the core personnel of the school needed a Bob to enter the venture on their side of the table to help manage the construction project.

An incredibly important note in understanding Bobs is that <u>many people who act like Bobs are not really on your side of the table</u>. They are on their own side. In my line of work, I see this often with the Owner/Architect relationship. While there are many honorable and reputable architectural firms that I have had the privilege to work with, there is no shortage of firms who are quick to cover their mistakes in unprincipled ways. If something is designed incorrectly, they are quick to ask the contractor for a "tradeoff" wherein the contractor finds a way to lower his cost in one part of the job in order to add the money to correct the faulty design in another. These unscrupulous firms are not on the owner's side, but on their own side in order to maintain the client's business.

At my company, we have a saying: "It's not about being right, it's about getting it right." You are far more likely to find partners who embody that saying when they are on your side of the table than when they are on their own side. In my field, architects are often resistant to the growing field of Construction Management – wherein the owner selects a firm based on merit *before* a project begins in order to serve as the management arm of the business/ entity. The firm then *oversees* the bidding and construction of the project but is firmly on the same side of the table as the owner. Since the construction manager is not the general contractor, there is no "windfall" of money, nor any other incentive to prevent the construction manager from pointing out any problems in design or construction. They are a Bob. It is imperative that you find Bobs for your side of the table—regardless of the industry you are in.

"SAGES" ARE INVALUABLE

The other type of partner I insist on having on my side of the table is what we call a "Sage." The term itself means "a profoundly wise person" and it conjures up imagery of a trustworthy old veteran in your field. Sages are likely the most valuable people you can put on your team because they typically join the team because they want to, not because they have to. Because of this, they are typically low-cost high-output team members.

My business partner is a retired Air Force Colonel. He spent 27 years in the service, overseeing thousands of people, billions of dollars in construction, and wound up with more degrees than Fahrenheit. Had he desired to venture into almost any area of corporate America upon retirement, he would have been compensated handsomely. However, instead, he moved home and saw an opportunity to use his experience and expertise to serve others. He worked with our local school district to spearhead a Jr. ROTC program at the high school. He spends his time working for the school because he *wants* to. He is a Sage.

In my line of work, a Sage is typically a retired construction superintendent with many years of experience. He/she does not *want* to work 40 hours a week and does not require salary or benefits commensurate with his/her experience because he/she merely *wants* to continue to be involved in construction by helping others. For a school official, a Sage might be a retired superintendent. For a hospital administrator, depending on the need, it may be a retired facilities manager or former surgeon.

Whatever a Sage is for your line of work it is imperative that you find one and seat them next to you at the table.

THE ROAD TO SUCCESS

At one time or another, we are all thrust into positions of responsibility that are not equal to our level of training or passion.

Often there are many sides and stakeholders involved. The best way to ensure your success is to make sure that, when you look around the table, you are confident that the people on your side are skilled, looking out for your best interests, and capable of managing the issue or project in a way that minimizes the impact to your (or your employees') day-to-day responsibilities. If the right people are on your side of the table, you will have won before the project starts.

About Aaron

Aaron R. Smith is a recognized expert in construction management services. He is the co-founder of Smith Hafeli, Inc., a full-range construction services firm, and is the CEO of *Fortune Construction Services*, a corporation designed to provide construction management services and consulting to clients in the government, healthcare, and educational sectors. He has participated in more than $100 million in construction projects, and works to consult and advise on building projects of all kinds.

Aaron has been invited to address the Illinois State Board of Education and the Illinois State Administrators Association on managing complex construction projects, and construction contracts.

For over a decade Aaron has been involved in the construction and renovation of buildings. With specializations in government contracting, healthcare facilities, and educational institutions, Aaron has developed a distinct reputation as a go-to authority on construction services from pre-construction to closeout.

Aaron is a Trustee at John A. Logan College in Carterville, IL giving him a unique understanding of what construction projects are like …on both sides of the table.

Aaron's M.B.A. is from Southern Illinois University, Carbondale – 15 miles from his Marion, IL home – and he continues to be an avid supporter of the Salukis.

Aaron is also a long-time member of Rotary International.

Visit Aaron at:

- Twitter: @aaronrsmith
- Email: aaron@smith-hafeli.com
- Website: www.smith-hafeli.com

CHAPTER 7

STAY THE COURSE– EMBRACE THE JOURNEY

BY AMY BANOCY

Hello friends and welcome to my chapter! I'm so glad you're here! You're likely reading this book because:

a) You've started a business, or you're committed to personal growth and feel stuck because you're not "successful yet."
    or
b) You're merely thinking about these things, having not acted yet, because the thought of failure scares your breakfast out of you, and you're hoping this book will provide the magic sauce to avoiding failure.

If neither of those is the case, maybe you're reading this book because, like me, you devour every book that may make you a better version of yourself and anything with the amazing Jack Canfield on the cover. Whatever the reason, I'm glad you're here! I hope you're cozied up in your favorite spot, with a cup of coffee or glass of bubbly in hand, because things are about to get fun!

I'm about to drop one of the biggest secrets to success right here, right now. Are you ready? Take a sip of that beverage, grab a pen and paper and get ready to have your life transformed in a single thought. Here it is friends:

"Along your road to success, in life and in business, YOU ARE GOING TO HIT ROADBLOCKS, AND YOU WILL ALSO EXPERIENCE FAILURE."

I know, it's a bit harsh, but here is the amazing part…

YOU HAVE THE POWER TO MAKE WHAT YOU DESIRE OUT OF EVERY SINGLE FAILURE AND BUMP IN THE ROAD!

How incredible is that? You can (and hopefully will, after reading this chapter) know to expect these could-be deterrents, make the most of each situation, and use the strategies I provide, to stay the course.

When I jumped into entrepreneurship, I had no idea what challenges I would face. I had taken a leap of faith (as most entrepreneurs do!) and partnered with a skincare company in the direct selling channel. I recognized that the products were life-changing, the brand had massive potential, and I simply didn't want to miss out. Outside of that, all I knew, was that I was excited and wanted to shout it from the rooftops. Can anyone relate?

I had huge goals for the first year and focused on only that. I have always been a glass ¾ full kind of gal, and I was certain this wasn't going to be any different. Well, the Universe had other plans and wanted to shake things up a bit. Little did I know, that when I would start telling people about my business, some would actually respond with negativity and criticism! I know, can you believe it? I heard things like, "What do you think you're doing?" and "You have no experience in that industry." and "Let's see where you are in a few months." (… all said with an insane amount of cynicism). I also had no idea of the roadblocks I would face, such as website issues, sold out inventory and people quitting. Well, I showed all those naysayers, and continue to do so every single day, as I build my empire. You guys, this is YOUR DREAM. Nobody else is going to build it for you. If you truly want whatever it is you are working toward, you're going to have to do just that, WORK! And one major piece of the work is: STAYING THE COURSE.

All right, so now that you have had a minute to digest all of that, take a sip of that delicious beverage and let's talk about HOW you can be prepared to face failure and those inevitable bumps in the road. And even more important, let's look at how to make sure these things don't keep you from finishing what you've started! Based on my own experiences in building businesses and growing massively in my personal life, here are my five tips to ensuring you STAY THE COURSE toward your goals and dreams.

<u>Fair Warning:</u> Results may be drastic, but will take work and will not be easy.

#1 – EMBRACE THE ZIG-ZAG

It is so important to recognize that when events, people or perhaps our own actions, take us off our course toward success, that they are likely happening for a reason. Not only do they serve a purpose, they are even occurring at that particular time, **on purpose.** I know to some, this may seem a bit crazy, but it's the truth, people. It is important to remember that every path to success and greatness looks different, but the one thing they have in common is that they're never a direct straight line. There will be ups and downs, as well as curves in different directions. In life and in business, there will be setbacks and the best way to handle them, is to get ahead of them. Expect they will happen and learn from them.

I experienced growth year-over-year during my first five years in business. You guys, you can imagine I was flying high with this excitement! Well, Year Six hit like a tornado, and it was not so pretty! Business was flat, *something I never thought would happen*. Yes, I know, I was a bit naive.

Thankfully, in those moments, I realized I had a choice to make. I could accept the situations at hand, grow from them and muster on, or I could throw in the towel and give up. Since "give up" is not in my vocabulary (and I assume it's not in yours either), you know which path I chose. I looked at what I could do as the leader of this organization, to bring it back together. I strategized with my team, dissected what wasn't working, and together, we were able to tweak some practices that weren't serving our customers or us. We put new systems in place and began to get back on track.

I am now so grateful for those tough times. They taught me that I could not become complacent, simply because we had such early success. I now have regular check-ins with myself and my team to evaluate what's working well and what changes need to be made in order to experience continued growth. When you find that things don't seem to be "on track," take a moment and embrace the pause. Think about what you can do to better understand the situation and how you can grow from it. There is most certainly a lesson in everything, even if you can't see it at the time.

#2 – SHUSH SELF-LIMITING BELIEFS AND PRACTICE EMPOWERED THINKING

Oh, this is one of my favorites, especially when I'm speaking to women. Many times we are subconsciously pushing ourselves off-course, simply by allowing our limiting beliefs to take over. These beliefs, which we have developed throughout our lives based on our upbringing, our environment and our experiences, can have a tremendous effect on our psyche, potentially causing a downward spiral in our journey. When someone in my sales organization would suddenly decide they didn't want to do the work necessary to build a successful business, I used to let that frustration turn into self-sabotaging thoughts. Thoughts such as, "Maybe I'm not a good leader" or "If everyone keeps quitting, I'll never be successful" were stemming from my limiting beliefs around not being good enough.

Do you think that had a positive effect on my business? Of course not! You guys, these inner negative thoughts can completely demonize us and take us off track, if we let them! In order to power through and be successful, I had to recognize what was happening and course correct this habit. Once I understood that someone else's decision had nothing to do with me and that it only had meaning once I gave it meaning, I realized I held the power! Our beliefs impact our habits, which in turn, impact our outcomes. Knowing this, you can now understand why limiting beliefs can have a negative impact on the positive outcomes you desire.

The great news is that you can consciously change this pattern! Shifting your limiting beliefs starts with an awareness of where those ideas come from. Once you have that awareness, you have the power to rewrite those stories and reframe your beliefs. Through meditation and deep reflection, I discovered that my self-limiting belief of, "I am not good enough" came from lifelong feelings that I received more positive attention when I accomplished great things, in someone else's mind. That developed into a habit of perfectionism and a subconscious belief that what I was producing would never be good enough. Living with this belief system, I would never be "successful" because, in my mind, I'd already convinced myself that I wasn't worthy.

So, I made a conscious decision to start listening to my own empowered voice, rather than these other voices in my mind. I began repeating affirmations such as, "I am an incredible leader for my team" and "I attract people who want to work hard and build the life of their dreams." Once I shifted the beliefs, my habits and outcomes were changed for the better and my affirmations became my truth.

Another amazing thing happened as a result of this too. My team saw my belief shifting, which inspired them to do the same. Positive energy is contagious, so be sure you are always leading from the front and setting the example for your team. Right now, yes, right now, make a list of five empowered affirmations and begin repeating them multiple times a day. Your brain will begin to believe these statements and <u>so-will-you!</u>

#3 – NOURISH YOUR SOUL

I recently had a situation when I found myself less than excited about what I was creating. It was bringing me down, both mentally and physically. My autoimmune issues flared up, causing me immense pain and fatigue. My mind was cluttered and in a negative space more often than a positive one. Thankfully, being in a heightened state of my own awareness, I was able to recognize this more quickly than I would have in the past. One of my mentors then asked me one question that would change my patterns and most likely my life forever. "Have you been doing daily personal development, Amy?" she asked. Surprisingly, the answer was no! While I have always loved learning and honing my skills, I had a major ah ha moment right then, that knowledge and growth are actually what fuel my soul and my mind. Without them, I become lost and less excited. The fact that you are reading this book may mean you feel the same.

Since that conversation, I have changed my habits and made personal development a daily non-negotiable. Through personal development, we consciously seek out knowledge that will have a positive effect on our lives. Research shows us that when we are learning and growing, we naturally become motivated to accomplish more. The best part is that there are myriads of resources today, to help you work on personal growth. We have podcasts, videos, apps, and so much more at our disposal. As it's been said by many, in an age of this much information, ignorance is a choice, people! Find what speaks to you and make the time for this work every single day. My favorite time to soak in the greatness of others is while I'm exercising. I'll hop on the treadmill and turn on one of my favorite podcasts. This is a double whammy, as I'm exercising my mind and my body at the same time. Talk about a power move! Try it. I dare you!

#4 – HAVE AN INSANE AMOUNT OF PASSION FOR YOUR VISION

As I said earlier, this is YOUR dream, my friend—nobody else's! If you want to see it through, you must feel so passionate about it, that when you lose a client, regain a few pounds or spend the money you've been trying to save, that it's not the be-all-end-all for you! You've got to know WHY you are doing what you're doing. It will guide you through the ups and downs, the long days, the tireless work. I believe to my core that I'm meant to empower women to live to their fullest potential. I know it's my mission and what I was put on this Earth to do. I feel so fired up by this that I will not stop working toward my goal of serving these women, *no-matter-what!*

Because of my autoimmune diseases, I often have days where I face intense pain, brain fog, and fatigue. Thankfully, I've learned how to control this through diet, exercise, wellness and awareness of managing my energy levels. However, there are still times when giving up would be the easier option. It is in these moments that I dig deep into my heart and remember exactly why I'm doing the work. So, I ask you, do you have a clear vision for why you're doing the work? If so, be sure to keep it top-of-mind, especially during tough times when you want to quit. If not, I highly encourage you to take some time to look inward, peel back the layers of that "onion", discover your WHY and get 'crazy' passionate about it.

#5 – CELEBRATE EVERY WIN, ESPECIALLY THE SMALL ONES

It's no secret that the things worth having (YOUR BIG DREAMS!), do not come easy. If you haven't figured it out yet, you're going to work hard, and you're going to want to quit because it's the easier option! But if you're still reading this, I know you're not a quitter, right? So, one of the simplest and most fun ways to persevere is by giving yourself permission to celebrate the small wins along the way. Let's say you have a goal of adding 20 new clients. I recommend celebrating each time you add a new client and are closer to reaching your goal. When we reward ourselves, we want to work harder to earn the reward again, therefore propelling us forward and closer to the end goal. Now, I'm not saying go out and buy the most expensive, couture shoes you can find, when you land a new client or lose your first couple of pounds. Let's keep it realistic, friends, and save the big rewards for the bigger end goals. Personally, I love rewarding myself with a massage, manicure or pedicure. Can you tell I love spoiling myself?!?! As a wife, mom of three very active boys and business owner, sometimes my win for the day is making sure everyone is dressed and where they need to be. You know what, I'll take that and celebrate! Pour the bubbly, honey! We're winning!

Friends, there you have it. My five simple tips you can start implementing today, *to ensure you stay the course and reach your big goals and dreams.* As someone who has experienced many distractions, failures, and moments off course, I can attest to the fact that these strategies will help you along your journey to success. Remember, nobody's journey is a straight line. There will be and ups and downs, so embrace them, learn from them and consider them a gift. While you may not see their value at the time, everything is happening exactly as it should!

About Amy

Amy Banocy, CEO of Ignite Your Passion, may be a seasoned entrepreneur, but she definitely didn't think that would be her path. She, perhaps, like many of you, started behind a desk, working for others and helping them build their dreams, rather than her own. After years spent in a variety of toxic work environments, this Penn State graduate decided it was time to use her skill sets to create her own legacy and to help others find success for themselves.

Amy didn't make the decision to set out on her own without facing the looming fear of failure that we're all familiar with. However, she jumped in with both feet into the world of entrepreneurship by partnering with a #1 consumer products brand. Fast-forward several years, and she's simultaneously raised a family, built her own business, and gets to call herself the proud CEO of a million-dollar international organization, consisting of over 500 salespeople and leaders.

A self-proclaimed personal development enthusiast, Amy's passion for knowledge extends far. Her deep understanding of Emotional Intelligence (EI) has helped her grow as a mom, wife, friend, and a female entrepreneur. She loves teaching others how to maximize these EI skills and empowering women to live life to their fullest.

Today, Amy's passion is taking women on a transformational journey and helping them break through the limiting beliefs which may be holding them back. Her vision stretches beyond simply helping entrepreneurs hit their target numbers. For her, it's about teaching women how emotional intelligence helps foster a healthier lifestyle and results in stronger relationships and increased self-confidence. And also, how this comprehensive transformation, in return, can result in higher sales and an increase in profit or, in other words, entrepreneurial success.

When she's not using her energy to empower fellow female entrepreneurs, this born and raised 'Northern Virginia mama' to three can be found sipping coffee, reading a motivational book and daydreaming of white sandy beaches.

CHAPTER 8

FINDING THE SOUL OF YOUR SUCCESS:
HOW MISSION-DRIVEN BRANDING PUTS YOU AHEAD OF THE PACK

BY JW DICKS AND NICK NANTON

They had been best friends since they were kids – and, as adults, they had decided to go into business together. They opened one small ice cream shop that turned into a local sensation – ironically, because a sinus condition made it difficult for the one partner to taste anything. They pumped up the flavors in their frozen concoctions to such an extent that it clicked with the college crowd that frequented the area.

The store became instantly successful. On the first anniversary of its opening, the owners held a "Free Cone Day," where they gave away a free ice cream cone to every customer. That and a yearly film festival they sponsored helped make them a vital part of the community. Their local support mushroomed.

But money was still a huge problem – in the winter, there was more of it going out than coming in. They began to study brochures put out by the Small Business Administration that cost 20 cents apiece at the Post Office. They franchised a couple other stores in the region. They began selling pints of their ice cream flavors to local stores. And finally, they began to see some real money coming in.

That's when they began some soul-searching. These two guys had been almost-hippies who had grown up in the 60's, so they wanted their business to represent that spirit. They wanted to put their social mission at the center of everything they did. They wanted to always have what they called "the double dip" in place – profits and people.

They started with their own people. They put in place a policy that no employee's rate of pay would be greater than five times that of entry-level employees. In 1995, that meant entry-level employees were paid $12 hourly and the CEO could only be paid $150,000 annually.

Then they moved on to the world at large. At the end of each month, the two of them would ask of themselves and the company, how much had they improved the quality of life in the community?

As the company's need for capital increased, they resisted venture capitalist financing, which typically requires relinquishing significant control over the company. Instead, it sold stock to residents in the region, keeping the company in local hands. In 1985, it officially created a foundation, to which the company would contribute 7.5 percent of its pretax profits.

They also made social activism a critical aspect of their operations, putting into action such projects as:

- An original scoop shop made of recycled materials
- Creation of a "Green Team" in 1989, focusing on environmental education throughout the company
- A company bus equipped with solar panels
- The use of hormone-free milk in its products
- A commitment to reducing solid and dairy waste, recycling, and water and energy conservation at the company's facilities

Ben Cohen and Jerry Greenfield's Ben & Jerry's ice cream brand ended up with annual sales of over $250 million by the end of the 90's – and was sold to Unilever for over $325 million in 2000. Today, it's regarded as the top premium ice cream brand in the world – and, even though it's now owned by a giant corporation, it still continues to deliver on its social mission to this day.

Ben & Jerry's discovered the soul of their success by always making sure their business had a soul. No doubt such iconic flavors as Cherry Garcia and Chunky Monkey helped propel them to the top – but, just as importantly, it was also the company's bigger societal mission that encouraged people to both invest in them and buy their ice cream. A 1995 article put it this way:

> "As the stockholders made clear, their investment in this ice cream company has less to do with its profitability than how it goes about making its profits. What Ben & Jerry's offers its investors is the chance to buy into a company that reminds them of themselves. A company that is innovative and impassioned about its product, but also values-driven. A company with a freewheeling sense of humor, but also a serious commitment to its community. Business on a human scale, in other words..."[1]

Or, as co-founder Jerry Greenfield himself said, revealing the real secret of their brand:

> "...we knew that's what would separate Ben & Jerry's — even more than the great flavors, it was important for us to make our social mission a central part of the company."[2]

To really discover the soul of any business's success, it's necessary to have in place a strong mission that goes beyond the usual profit

---

1. Carlin, Peter. "Pure Profit: For Small Companies That Stress Social Values as Much as the Bottom Line, Growing Up Hasn't Been an Easy Task. Just Ask Ben & Jerry's, Patagonia and Starbucks." The Los Angeles Times, February 5, 1995.
2. Harrison, J.D. "When We Were Small: Ben & Jerry's." The Washington Post, May 14, 2014

motive that drives most entrepreneurs. When you're mission-driven, you have the opportunity to create a powerful and lasting brand that can continue to draw customers, grow profits and do good things for the world all at the same time.

Without that mission, however…?

Well, Unilever, the multinational conglomerate that bought the company in 2000, found out the answer to that question. After Ben and Jerry sold the business, the brand went into a slump because, first of all, the brand's true believers thought the founders had also sold out the company's mission – and second of all, that turned out to be largely true. Unilever effectively shut the founders out of any decision-making and also curtailed the do-gooder missions of the company. To them, all that stuff was just some kind of marketing ploy.

That's why, in 2004, when Walt Freese was named as Unilever's CEO, he quickly invited Ben and Jerry back into the fold to reinvigorate the company's mission – and, of course, the brand itself. Once that mission was again completely back on track, so was the company. How important is that mission to this day?

Well, in 2010, Jostein Solheim, a Unilever executive from Norway, became the new CEO of the company and had this to say about the transition:

> "The world needs dramatic change to address the social and environmental challenges we are facing. Values-led businesses can play a critical role in driving that positive change. We need to lead by example, and prove to the world that this is the best way to run a business. Historically, this company has been and must continue to be a pioneer to continually challenge how business can be a force for good and address inequities inherent in global business."[3]

---

3. "Division President: Jostein Solheim, Ben & Jerry's Homemade," FoodProcessing.com, http://www.foodprocessing.com/ceo/jostein-solheim/

In other words, in the case of Ben & Jerry's, the mission and the business were inseparable. Each made the other all the more powerful. It was the soul of their success.

MISSION-DRIVEN BRANDING: THE NEW PARADIGM

It used to be enough to make customers feel something – even if it didn't necessarily have a lot to do with your actual product or service.

It was "the Age of Emotion" for branding. In the words of Advertising Age:

> "Prompted by booms of products and prosperity, conspicuous consumption kicked into high gear, and logic wasn't enough. Your product had to make a prospective buyer feel something. A car was freedom on four wheels, jeans made you rebellious."[4]

Yes, branding used to be all about tugging the heartstrings. For example, back in the 1970's, the classic heartwarming Coke commercial featuring football player "Mean" Joe Greene throwing a kid his jersey would make a nation sigh and open another bottle of Coke. McDonalds' famous song-and-dance "You Deserve a Break Today" campaign would motivate families to give Mom the night off from cooking and go get some Big Macs, while Kodak would sell its cameras and film with sentimental family photos and a goofy Paul Anka jingle, "For the Times of Your Life."

Today? Because you can instantly take photos with your phone, Kodak is virtually out of business. The Coca-Cola Company is under fire for allegedly causing obesity and is desperate to repair the image of its signature product. And McDonalds? In 2013, when it began soliciting positive customer comments on Twitter,

---

4. Walker, Abbie. "Brands Need to Know Their Purpose and What They Aspire to Be," Advertising Age, February 24, 2014.

it instead got overwhelmed with tweeted horror stories from the public, leading the campaign to be dubbed "McFail."

Technology and the Internet have changed everything. That, in turn, means manufactured emotions delivered by an ad or a commercial will only get an organization so far these days. As the same Advertising Age article goes on to say, "Our brands ask consumers for what a person expects from his or her friends—loyalty, trust, attention, love, time—without putting in the reciprocally requisite work. In other words, brands need to reconsider their motivations and behaviors because no one is buying the be-our-friend act any longer." [5]

In other words, trying to manufacture an emotion without having anything real behind it just won't do the job for a business anymore.

That's why Mission-Driven Branding is a must for this day and age. When an organization genuinely takes on a mission and implements it inside and out, when it is consistent and authentic in pursuing that mission, that organization has a far greater chance of creating loyalty and trust – and of creating an authentic emotional response - than by constantly reinventing its appeal with gimmicky short-term marketing campaigns.

There are two huge factors in play today that are an enormous threat to any company trying to win over customers and clients with superficial marketing tactics:

1. There's too much information out there.

Abraham Lincoln famously said, "You can fool all the people some of the time, and some of the people all the time, but you cannot fool all the people all the time." That's never been more true than right this minute.

For example, a few years back, the Chik-fil-A restaurant

5. Walker.

chain was embroiled in a firestorm over its backing of anti-gay policies. At the time, a sweet-looking teenage girl rushed to the company's defense by writing earnest posts on her Facebook page detailing all of Chick-fil-A's wonderful qualities. But, because the Internet is the Internet, somebody quickly figured out that this girl's picture was licensed from a stock photo company - and the media presumed that Chick-Fil-A had most likely set up the fake account to manufacture support for its positions,[6] even with no real evidence to prove it.

In other words, whereas a brand might have been able to get away with these kinds of practices before, there is virtually no chance of it now. Even if Chick-fil-A hadn't put up the fake Facebook account, the Internet "jury" still found the company guilty by association. And this was far from an isolated case – right now, there are now millions of amateur "branding police" actively investigating which companies are trying to pull a fast one and which ones are being authentic.

The Mission-Driven company has a natural advantage in this punitive climate. When it stays true to its mission, an organization can't help but pass the "smell test" on the Internet and elsewhere. It earns respect rather than derision from its actions – and that respect boosts its brand above the competition.

2. There are too many choices out there.

With all the options out there for a consumer, and all things being equal, how is that person going to choose who to buy from? Or perhaps the bigger question is: Why would that person choose to buy from a certain company or individual over another? Being Mission-Driven gives your company

---

6. Johnson, Dave. "Did Chick-fil-A's PR use fake Facebook account?" CBSNews.com, July 30, 2012. http://www.cbsnews.com/news/did-chick-fil-as-pr-use-fake-facebook-account/

the answer to a customer's "Why." By defining how your brand uniquely serves the customer or society at large, you also define the positive role of your brand in that person's life.

Let's go back to a few of the brands we already talked about and see how their missions add value not only to the brands themselves, but also to a consumer's buying experience:

- If you want yummy ice cream and you want to make the world a better place, you buy from Ben & Jerry's.
- If you want a good chicken lunch or dinner and want to support a company that shares your values, you buy from Chick-fil-A.
- If you want a smartphone and want to buy from the company with the most innovative and stylish technology, you buy from Apple.

In each of the above cases, the company's mission gives the consumer a strong, concrete reason to buy from them – and to continue buying from them. There will always be plenty of premium ice cream brands, chicken restaurants and smartphone manufacturers to choose from – but Ben & Jerry's, Chick-fil-A and Apple all bring a whole lot more than their actual products to the consumer marketplace. No, their individual missions don't resonate with everyone – but they resonate strongly enough with a large enough base to keep their brands incredibly profitable and continually growing.

Again, being Mission-Driven is not really an option in today's marketplace - it's a necessity. As FastCoExist.com put it, "Today's brand must live and breathe through its core values in order to survive. Purpose is king, and there's no turning back."[7] And, in the words of Charles Schwab's

---

7. Blotter, Jennifer. "10 Ways Today's Purpose-Driven Brands Can Bring Their Core Values to Life," FastCoExist.com, October 14, 2013. http://www.fastcoexist.com/3019856/10-ways-todays-purpose-driven-brands-can-bring-their-core-values-to-life

executive vice president and CMO, Becky Saeger, "to be successful today, you must identify your company's purpose and execute like crazy."[8]

MISSION-DRIVEN BRANDING: HOW IT DELIVERS THE FIVE BIG "D'S"

We'd like to close this chapter by naming what we've identified as the "5 Big D's" - the 5 biggest benefits that a successful mission can bring to any brand:

- **DESIRABILITY**

The right mission attracts a fervent and loyal customer/client base all on its own. When that mission is organically attached to the brand in question, the brand not only attracts buyers, it also attracts quality employees who want to be a part of the brand's mission. Apple again is the best example of this principle in action, but there's no question the quality of Desirability applies to many, many other Mission-Driven brands as well, such as Disney, Patagonia, or Zappos.

- **DISTANCE**

Any brand faces the danger of losing its luster over time. Remember when Atari was the only gaming choice in American households? Or when you could find a Blockbuster video store in every strip mall in the neighborhood? In contrast, having a firm mission in place – and, just as importantly, continuing to make that mission relevant (imagine if Blockbuster had been the first to do what Netflix did) – almost guarantees consumer loyalty and an ongoing high profile in the marketplace, allowing a brand to truly go the distance.

- **DEPENDABILITY**

A mission helps a brand retain a consistent identity in the public's mind over the long haul. That consistency is important

---

8. Adamson, Allen. "Define Your Brand's Purpose, Not Just Its Promise." Forbes, November 11, 2009.

to developing trust and likeability with clients/customers and keeping them coming back for more. Walmart's "Always the Lowest Price" mission, for example, drives a constant stream of bargain-driven consumers through its doors, because those consumers know the retailer has a high degree of dependability.

- **DIRECTION**

A mission empowers a brand to focus on what it does best and provide a strong direction for the company as a whole. For instance, companies like Google and Apple understand they have a mandate to continue to deliver innovative technology that improves people's lives. That mandate, in turns, drives how they do business over the long haul and forces them to concentrate on the direction that defines them in terms of public perception.

- **DIFFERENTIATION**

Finally, Mission-Driven branding creates a powerful differentiation in the marketplace in contrast to the competition. Ben & Jerry's had that differentiation when they first began as a homegrown socially-aware business – and they quickly lost it when the brand became just another acquisition by a multinational corporation, Unilever. For those few years, they were just another ice cream brand – and it was easy for their formerly fervent fans to simply pick another ice cream if it was cheaper or more convenient. A mission makes a company more than just another merchant or service provider – it transforms it into something much more meaningful and substantial, a business that truly stands out from the pack.

Of course, we've cherry-picked a lot of successful brands in this chapter to demonstrate the power of Mission-Driven branding. You the reader might rightly ask, "Well, yes, a mission works for big players like Apple and Google, but what real difference does it make to most companies?"

Well, we're glad you asked (even if we were the ones doing the asking for you) – because, it turns out, there is actually a concrete way to demonstrate the overall and overwhelming advantage of Mission-Driven branding.

In 2011, Havas Media Labs, one of the leading global communications and marketing groups, began compiling what they called the "Meaningful Brands Index." For the first time, a detailed analysis of companies that were Mission Driven in one way or another (through CSR (Corporate Social Responsibility) policies, sustainability, community giving, cause marketing, etc.) was done to determine just how this kind of brand activity affected their actual business.

The result? In the 2013 survey, the most recent one as of this writing, the so-called Meaningful Brands outperformed the stock market by an incredible 120%.[9]

Umair Haque, director of Havas Media Labs, had this to say as an explanation of the amazing success of Mission-Driven brands: "People aren't irrational in what they expect. They don't want perfect lives—but they do want better lives. What we consistently find is that institutions don't meet their expectations in real human terms. When they do find companies that are willing to benefit them, they're really happy doing business with them."[10]

And that to us is definitely the Soul of Success!

---

9. Dill, Kathryn. "Google, Samsung, Microsoft Head A Tech-Dominated List of The Most 'Meaningful' Brands," Forbes, June 14, 2013.
10. Ibid.

About JW

JW Dicks, Esq., is a Business Development Attorney, a *Wall Street Journal* Best-Selling Author®—who has authored over 47 books—a 5-time Emmy® Award-winning Executive Producer and a Broadway Show Producer.

JW is an XPrize Innovation Board member, Board Member of the National Retirement Council, Chairman of the Board of the National Academy of Best-Selling Authors®, Board Member of the National Association of Experts, Writers and Speakers®, and a Board Member of the International Academy of Film Makers®.

JW is the CEO of DNAgency, an Inc. 5000 Multimedia Company that represents over 3000 clients in 63 countries. He has been quoted on business and financial topics in national media such as *USA Today, The Wall Street Journal, Newsweek, Forbes, CNBC.com*, and *Fortune Magazine Small Business*.

Considered a Thoughtleader® and curator of information, JW has co-authored books with legends like Jack Canfield, Brian Tracy, Tom Hopkins, Dr. Nido Qubein, Steve Forbes, Richard Branson, Michael Gerber, Dr. Ivan Misner, and Dan Kennedy. He is the Publisher of *ThoughtLeader® Magazine.*

JW has appeared on business television shows airing on ABC, NBC, CBS, and FOX affiliates around the country and coproduces and syndicates a line of franchised business television shows such as *Success Today, Wall Street Today, Hollywood Live,* and *Profiles of Success.*

JW and his wife of 47 years, Linda, have two daughters, and four granddaughters. He is a sixth-generation Floridian and splits his time between his home in Orlando and his beach house on Florida's west coast.

About Nick

An Emmy Award-Winning Director and Producer, Nick Nanton, Esq., produces media and branded content for top thought leaders and media personalities around the world. Recognized as a leading expert on branding and storytelling, Nick has authored more than two dozen Best-Selling books (including the *Wall Street Journal* Best-Seller, *StorySelling™*) and produced and directed more than 50 documentaries, earning 5 Emmy Awards and 18 nominations. Nick speaks to audiences internationally on the topics of branding, entertainment, media, business and storytelling at major universities and events.

As the CEO of DNA Media, Nick oversees a portfolio of companies including: The Dicks + Nanton Agency (an international agency with more than 3000 clients in 65 countries), Dicks + Nanton Productions, Ambitious.com and DNA Films. Nick is an award-winning director, producer and songwriter who has worked on everything from large scale events to television shows with the likes of Steve Forbes, Ivanka Trump, Sir Richard Branson, Rudy Ruettiger (inspiration for the Hollywood Blockbuster, *RUDY*), Brian Tracy, Jack Canfield (*The Secret*, creator of the *Chicken Soup for the Soul* Series), Michael E. Gerber, Tom Hopkins, Dan Kennedy and many more.

Nick has been seen in *USA Today, The Wall Street Journal, Newsweek, BusinessWeek, Inc. Magazine, The New York Times, Entrepreneur® Magazine, Forbes, FastCompany,* and has appeared on ABC, NBC, CBS, and FOX television affiliates across the country as well as on CNN, FOX News, CNBC, and MSNBC from coast to coast.

Nick is a member of the Florida Bar, a member of The National Academy of Television Arts & Sciences (Home to the EMMYs), Co-founder of The National Academy of Best-Selling Authors®, and serves on the Innovation Board of the XPRIZE Foundation, a non-profit organization dedicated to bringing about "radical breakthroughs for the benefit of humanity" through incentivized competition, best known for its Ansari XPRIZE which incentivized the first private space flight and was the catalyst for Richard Branson's Virgin Galactic.

Nick also enjoys serving as an Elder at Orangewood Church, working with Young Life, Downtown Credo Orlando, Entrepreneurs International and rooting for the Florida Gators with his wife, Kristina, and their three children, Brock, Bowen and Addison.

Learn more at:
- www.NickNanton.com
- www.CelebrityBrandingAgency.com

CHAPTER 9

THE RICH HAVE SECRETLY STOPPED AGING...

AND GUESS WHAT? YOU STILL ARE

BY DR. MICHAEL GRAY

Just a few years ago wealthy A-list celebrities, billionaires, and leading anti-aging scientists gathered in southern California, by invitation only, at the home of a well-known billionaire. This was a secret meeting reserved only for celebrities, the very affluent, and elite. The celebrities paid $100,000 each to learn about successful youthful living and how to de-age the cells of the human body. The meeting was profound and addressed the "Secret of Opting Out of Old Age." That exclusive meeting focused on breakthrough scientific discoveries that actually reverse the aging process within the human body. What they learned and discovered in those two days was secret, and only the Rich and Famous could afford. When the meeting was adjourned each attendee left with the Secret to Successful Youthful Living. That's just not fair! The rich aren't just getting richer, now they are getting younger.

The results of that meeting were profound and would change the world of medicine as we know it. The scientists revealed that years, even decades of aging can now be reversed. Injuries once thought to be crippling could now be healed. Even more astonishing is they learned how growing younger biologically is within their grasp. Staying youthful, sharp, energized for decades longer is now more probable than ever thought possible.

What knowledge did they learn? Was it worth the $100,000 price of admission? Would they share their secret? Is the Secret real or just hype? Is the Secret of Successful Youthful Living within the grasp of the average man or woman? What if you could grow biologically younger and prolong the human youth span? What if you were 70 years old but felt 40? Are you willing to accept that getting old and feeling bad are just part of the aging process? I am here to tell you that with these recent scientific breakthroughs in regenerative medicine... old age is now OPTIONAL. The "human youth span" can be extended by 20, 30, even 40 years. Old Age can be reversed, and physical decline can be delayed. How is that possible?

Just imagine for a moment. What if you could replace all the old worn-out damaged cells in your body with fresh young cells. Is it safe to assume that you would feel much younger, look much younger, act much younger? Not exactly! Literally you would be much younger. Take for example a legendary NFL quarterback who goes from "washed up" at the age of 36 to having a record-setting MVP season just one year later at 37. How about an aging NBA Superstar who tried stem cell therapy. After injuring his knee this superstar thought his career was over. Then he decided to try stem cell therapy. His results: He played three more years, at the highest level and today is one of the NBA's all-time scoring leaders. Both refused to accept physical limitations and sought stem cell therapy to extend their careers and rejuvenate their aging broken bodies.

The Secret to Successful Youthful Living seems to center around the topic of regenerative medicine and more specifically "The Stem Cell Revolution." Undoubtedly, you may have heard about stem cells. Years ago scientist were able to clone sheep and some of those 'Affluent Rich' could even have their favorite pet cloned. Well, you might be surprised to learn that stem cells are increasingly being used in medicine. "Regenerative medicine is a revolutionary approach to treating many degenerative diseases and injuries," explains Kristin Comella, Ph.D., Chief Science Officer of American Stem Cell Centers of Excellence. "It is continually growing, and includes a variety of techniques, such as stem cell therapy, to harness your own body's natural healing mechanisms." Stem Cell Therapy is that new field of medicine that has even the wealthiest seeking….The Secret to Successful Youthful Living.

Let's examine the phenomenon of stem cells. Stem cells are products of conception. They are just one component of many regenerative tissues that surround and protect the fetus while in the womb and at the same time grow human tissue and organs. These primitive cells create a complete human being in nine months. All 220 different cell-types of the human body are grown and developed in mothers' wombs by the creative genius of stem cells. Once the job of creating a human being is complete, the stem cells take on new responsibilities. They then become responsible for repairing and replacing damaged and dying cells.

Stem cells exist in every tissue of our bodies and their main function is to maintain and repair damaged cells. Our bodies are constantly trying to repair dying and damaged human cells by releasing stem cells from our bone marrow into the blood stream. The stem cell's sole purpose is to seek out and repair damaged and dying tissue. This is what happens when your body repairs itself naturally. Instead of stitching and replacing body parts... or flooding your system with drugs, your body is programmed to actually repair itself, cell by cell, organ by organ. The amazing human body is continually recreating itself with the help of stem cells. This is a constant process that never ends until the day we die. How often does your body replace its organs? Your lungs recreate themselves every 2-3 weeks, your colon every 2-3 days, your skin every 14 days, your red blood cells every four months, your heart muscle 24/7, your liver is 100% new every 5 months, and your joint and cartilage cells are constantly renewing. Wow! Pretty amazing.

Let's explore the steps of recreation, or in other words, rejuvenation. <u>Step one:</u> When your body is injured, or cells grow old and begin to die, your body sends out SOS signals. These signals cause an army of stem cells to race to the scene and suppress inflammation. This mixture of cells is a "regenerative soup" which contains cytokines which are very good at reducing inflammation and modulating your body's immune response. Large amounts of growth factors, cell adhesion molecules, etc. are also present in the "regenerative soup." If the the body needs repair, tissue repair occurs. <u>Step two:</u> Once on the scene of the injury or cell death, stem cells transform themselves into BRAND-NEW cells. These replace the old damaged ones and you're good as new. Stem cells are so smart, all you have to do is turn them loose. They float around to different areas of the body and fix whatever damaged cells they come in contact with. In fact, right now as you sit there reading this information, your stem cells are flowing through your blood stream searching for aging and damaged cells to replace.

The only drawback to the above scenario is the fact that if you are 60 years of age, your body's output of repair stem cells drops by 85% leaving only 15% and by the age of 80 stems cells numbers drop by 95% leaving only 5% left to repair all the damaged and dying cells in your body. Bone marrow stem cells get lazy with age and there are fewer cells produced to carry out the role of rebuilding. At one point in time our cells which are old, tired, and weak literally start breaking down faster than our bodies can repair themselves. This is what ultimately leads to death.

The dilemma becomes how to slow down and even reverse the aging process? Can we cheat death? Can we stop Father Time? Common sense tells us that if we want to live longer, be more active, and have pain-free lives, then we must learn how to increase the number of stem cells and supercharge the growth factors in our bodies. We must open the floodgates and let that stream of specialized allograph tissue and stem cells join the fight against aging.

How do we release this amazing power? What's the secret? Is there a secret laboratory in a deep vault in the desert of California where scientists are developing the most powerful drug ever imagined? A drug so powerful and amazing that it can regenerate every cell in the human body? No! It's not hidden in some secret location. The secret has been in plain sight for 100 years. The secret cure is found in the miraculous and amazing bodies of pregnant mothers – within the amniotic fluid and the umbilical cord tissues. The power that created a human being in nine months is stored in those tissues and is waiting to be released. Once the army of stem cells enters the fight, miracles happen. Knees and hips are repaired. Diseased inflamed organs are rejuvenated and regenerated. A youthful feeling returns. Life feels good again. Instead of relying on extra cups of coffee to stay energized, you would be naturally energized like you were decades ago. Instead of looking at life and thinking of all the things you can't do anymore, you can start making plans to do all the things you love to do. Like a walk on the beach, a round of golf with your friends, playing with your grandkids, or simply preserving your precious independence and mobility. Your energy levels, your heart, your joints, your organs, your brain, your skin and your whole outlook on life are profoundly improved. You get outstanding results with zero complications or rejection. You have experienced **The Secret of Successful Youthful Living.**

Those who decide to try regenerative stem cell therapy usually acquire six common characteristics of **Successful Youthful Living:**

- First, they are essentially pain free.
- Second, they sleep more restfully and for more hours.
- Third, they are more active.
- Fourth, they have a more positive outlook on life.

- Fifth, they are able to sort through negative false information and make the smart decisions regarding their health care.
- Sixth, they are more appreciative of their new-found freedom.

What else can I expect after stem cell therapy? You'll find yourself growing younger instead of older. You'll work longer hours and take fewer naps. "You'll Never Send Me to a Nursing Home" will be your mentality. You'll not only feel younger, but trillions of the cells in your body will actually be younger. How about never needing a walker? How about being 80 and feeling 50? Even better, how about growing biologically younger, and staying youthful, lean, sharp, sexy, and energized for decades longer than you ever thought possible. Too good to be true? The cat is out of the bag. The secret is now available for all to experience.

Stem cell therapy is no longer just for the high-paid athletes or rich celebrities...it has become more mainstream.
~ The Miami Herald

In a world where doctors and surgeons play "God", isn't it better to help the human body repair itself naturally? No longer is surgery to replace or remove body parts the only option. When all is said and done, allograph amniotic and/or umbilical stem cell infusion to replace your old, damaged, dying cells with new vibrant young tissue is **The Secret of Successful Youthful Living.**

About Dr. Michael

Dr. Michael Gray has spent thirty-five years consulting with, treating, and educating over 25,000 patients. He has devoted his life and career to educating people on how to live safer, happier, successful, youthful, and healthier lives. He takes great joy knowing he has helped people become more successful and achieve active pain-free lives. Born in El Paso, Texas he lived in an abusive alcoholic home. After years of negativism and suppression, his life was forever changed when two teenagers (John King and George Vaughn) befriended him. Their friendship lifted him out of that suppressive abusive environment. Their kindness and several Christian mentors inspired him to serve his fellow man.

After graduating from high school, he boarded a bus for Nashville, Tennessee and spent two weeks in sales training for The Southwestern Bible Company. Every night he listened to Earl Nightingale and learned from the master salesman. He looks back on his days of knocking door-to-door as "life changing." As his self-esteem grew so did his confidence. Soon he adopted the mentality: "Don't Tell Me I Can't Do It!" That philosophy led to an unending drive to become more accomplished and educated. Dr. Gray understood that knowledge was his key to success. He attended Lubbock Christian University where he worked three jobs as a full-time student. He holds a Bachelor of Arts in Education and a Master of Educational Administration from Harding University. Cleveland University awarded him a Doctor of Chiropractic and thus began his quest to help improve the health of patients.

Dr. Gray currently is the CEO of Keller Disc and Spine, a multidisciplinary integrated practice. He speaks at more than thirty seminars a year on a variety of specialized health topics. He loves to teach people how to become more active and pain-free with Regenerative Medicine including Stem Cell Therapy. Dr. Gray serves as the Official Doctor for The World Outdoor 3-Wall Ball Tournament and treats five of the top professional racquetball players in the world. Several USA Olympic team members call Dr. Gray their doctor. Currently his practice is devoted to regenerative and anti-aging medicine.

Dr. Gray met and married his wife Nancy Work while attending Harding University. They have lived in the Dallas Ft. Worth area for 36 years and have raised five children: Heather, Austin, Jordan, Kellee, and Wendy. All five of his children have college degrees from four different Christian Universities. He and Nancy have been married for 46 years and currently reside in Keller, Texas.

Dr. Gray acknowledges Dan Kennedy, Earl Nightingale, Zig Ziglar, Dr. Ben Altadonna, Bill Glazer, and Dr. Pete Fernandez for their contribution to his professional development and success.

Dr. Michael Gray can be contacted at:

- Keller Disc and Spine
  1710 Rufe Snow, Keller, Texas 76248
- Email: Xgenmed1@gmail.com

CHAPTER 10

HEALTHY AGING SUCCESS OR SABOTAGE
WHAT'S DRIVING YOUR AGING STORY?

BY KAY VAN NORMAN

"I'm fine with becoming frail and dependent with age," said *no-one,* ever! Yet, nursing homes are filled with *accidental* residents who fully intended to age well but failed to create a plan and take action. Ultimately, what robs you of independence and health isn't age. It's the gap between your intentions for aging well and your actions.

People often fear a life-changing illness or injury will derail health, yet after 25 years as a healthy aging specialist, I know it's most often the small choices made day after day – compounded over time – that sabotage wellbeing.

So, I'm not offering health advice in this chapter. It's everywhere! In fact, you could probably tell me what you should do to stay healthy – eat right, exercise, don't smoke, don't run with scissors. Instead, I'm sharing hard-won insights on how your attitudes and expectations, what I call – *aging scripts* – drive daily choices, creating a big gap between knowing what you should do and actually doing it!

This chapter illuminates your current aging path and helps you build a roadmap for lifelong health. It will:

- reveal what you're personally thinking, saying, and doing about aging well.
- illustrate how personal beliefs impact health.
- outline the *Vitality Portfolio®* approach – a simple 3-step-plan to help you build and sustain lifelong vitality.

The journey starts with a few simple questions.

EXPECTATIONS AND HIDDEN SCRIPTS

Do you expect to be healthy and active through your full lifespan?

When I give keynote speeches, most people answer yes to that question. But when I ask audiences to stand and either remain standing or sit down based on answers to yes or no questions, surprising gaps emerge between intentions and actions.

Do you expect to be as strong and agile five years from now as you are today?

Most people remain standing.

Do you strength train at least twice a week on a regular basis?

About 70% of the audience sits down. That's a major gap. Because unless you're challenging your muscles regularly, I guarantee you're losing strength – at an average rate of 1-1½ % per year after about age 30. Do the math to see you can easily lose half your strength by age 70!

In the past two weeks have you made a joking or serious reference to your physical performance being diminished by age, or to having a senior moment when forgetting a name or a fact?

This question reveals a hidden negative script, and takes out the majority of those still standing.

Would you still be standing?

After ten simple questions, very few audience members remain standing whose internalized expectations and actions are aligned to support healthy aging. That's surprisingly consistent around the world, from executives at seminars to retirees looking for healthy aging advice.

EXPECTATIONS WORK FOR OR AGAINST YOU

What you think and say about aging matters because to age well your beliefs must consistently work for rather than against you. Hundreds of research studies describe how aging attitudes and expectations impact outcomes. I've read most of them. But two personal experiences imprinted this concept in my mind and heart.

(1). Eldo's story

At age 82, Eldo (my horseback riding buddy) fell off a haystack and broke his back and neck. Friends were devastated – convinced he was finished. But when I walked into his hospital room the first thing he said was, "I can't believe I messed up my whole *bleeping* (use your imagination) summer of riding." Amazing! He didn't get the memo saying he couldn't recover – at his age – so was just angry he was going to miss a summer of riding in the beautiful Montana mountains!

With an ageless mindset, every decision Eldo made and action he took focused on achieving fullest recovery. He asked for what he needed from healthcare, family, and friends. He hosted a 4th of July barbeque two days after he got out of the hospital, signifying - *don't count me out, I'm still part of this riding group!* Seven weeks later he called to report his doctor cleared him to ride and we headed to the mountains.

Eldo re-built his strength and stamina with progressively longer rides until two months later he rode our annual 24-mile loop in Yellowstone National Park. I was exhausted. He was fine! At 89 years old, Eldo continues his passion for riding. His positive expectations worked *for* rather than *against* him. Without them, his story would be very different.

(2). Ruth's story

85-year-old Ruth enjoyed life and was always open to new experiences. When she learned I was a professional dancer, she attended every dress rehearsal night so we could sit together when I wasn't on stage, discussing styles of dance from hip hop to ballet and the meaning of different choreography. My favorite memory of her was after a particularly abstract piece where the dancer draped over the back of, off to the side, and slithered around and under a chair. I asked her opinion and she just smiled and said, "I've felt the very same way waiting in a doctor's office before." I loved Ruth.

Then she fell and broke her hip. This hospital visit was very different. She talked about her kids and grandkids and what a good life she'd had. Cheerfully, I described the road to recovery – therapy and back to exercise class. She continued her life review.

Finally, after several exchanges – me looking forward, her looking back - Ruth patted me on the knee, looked directly into my eyes and said, "Kay, honey, I've never known anyone my age to recover from a broken hip." Believe me, I tried with great conviction to convince her otherwise, but I knew she was in serious trouble.

I've studied how expectations drive outcomes, but was still stunned when Ruth was gone in two weeks. She believed with every fiber of her being that she couldn't recover from a broken hip at her age – and simply wasn't willing to live the life she envisioned as her destiny.

AGING SCRIPTS CONTROL YOU

If you get nothing else out of this chapter – please know with absolute certainty that to age with vitality you must examine and deliberately control the aging scripts running in your head. They form your personal beliefs about aging, so they drive behaviors and outcomes.

No-one ages in a bubble. We learn aging scripts in family, in community, and in culture-things like:

> *It's normal to become frail with age,*
> *Now that I'm 65 I should make my life smaller,*
> *I can't recover from a broken hip.*
> > *OR*
> *I can prevent frailty and retain independence,*
> *Age doesn't define who I am or what I'm capable of,*
> *I can claim vitality and live fully, in spite of challenges.*

Whether you're consciously aware of your aging scripts or not, your subconscious mind uses them to choose your aging path. You have to actively work to expose 'ageist' beliefs that sabotage health.

CREATE A PERSONAL *VITALITY PORTFOLIO*®

I've spent the past ten years carefully developing the *Vitality Portfolio*® approach to lifelong health. Part of the motivation has been my own desire to continue dancing and horseback riding and enjoying my family and meaningful work throughout my entire life. The other part has been watching aging go very badly for people I love – unnecessarily so – and wanting to do what I can to keep others from stumbling over the most common roadblocks to lifelong health.

The familiar structure of a financial portfolio – make a plan, balance assets, and make regular deposits – works beautifully for creating a personal vitality plan. The *Vitality Portfolio®* approach will help reveal your personal aging scripts and build a practical healthy aging roadmap in three simple steps:

1. Make a vitality plan
2. Balance vitality assets
3. Make regular deposits

Step 1: Make a Vitality Plan

How long do you expect to live? Surprisingly, most people seem to have a number in their head when asked. Consider your number. Whether it's 70+ or 100+ think about where you want to live, what you want to be able to do, and what you need to make that happen. People often spend more time planning a vacation (where, what, how) than they do planning their life! Making a vitality plan helps you set and reach your goals for lifelong health.

Step 2: Balance Vitality Assets

After years of observation and experience I identified three primary asset groups that, when combined, consistently create a strong foundation for lifelong health. The Vitality Portfolio® model (see Figure 1) illustrates these mission-critical assets:

- Wellness– six dimensions of health
- Core – ageless thinking and resilience
- Functional – strength, mobility, and endurance

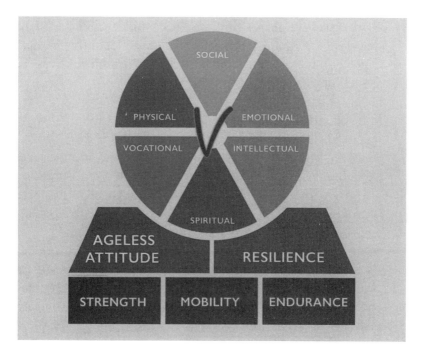

Figure 1: *Vitality Portfolio®* Model - © Brilliant Aging, 2019

My website: www.kayvannorman.com offers details, but here are the basics!

a. **Wellness Assets:** Consider your life's balance by visualizing the six dimensions of health – physical, social, emotional, intellectual, spiritual, and vocational – as spokes on a wheel. Consider how many regular deposits you make into each dimension (spoke), then draw your Wellness Wheel. Yes, it looks more like a pie but Wellness Pie seems like an oxymoron!

Are some spokes really large (lots of deposits) while others barely exist? Are you missing an entire spoke? Life constantly changes so dimensions overlap, ebb, and flow through life. The Wellness Wheel simply provides a visual reminder to support optimal health through a richly balanced life.

b. Core Assets: Ageless thinking and resilience are absolutely essential for lifelong vitality. The power of attitudes and expectations to uplift and enrich, or diminish, lives is astonishing.

For example, years ago people with disabilities were institutionalized with no expectations or hope for a future. The disability movement dramatically changed attitudes and expectations and now young people with severe disabilities are given resources, tools, and encouragement to triumph over adversity. They receive a steady diet of positive beliefs and resilience training, and accomplish amazing things!

By contrast, older adults with disabilities are most often given resources and tools to cope with, rather than overcome, challenges. Picture healthcare's focus when a 40-year-old has a stroke – it's for fullest recovery; while getting a 75-year-old stroke survivor home and comfortable is commonly viewed as a success. There's a profoundly different mindset between overcoming and coping, resulting in profoundly different outcomes.

Aging well isn't just for people without health challenges! Remember Eldo? He reclaimed his life after a severe injury by rejecting aging stereotypes, demanding fullest recovery, and taking action!

Immerse yourself in a culture of possibilities, associate with others who believe in positive aging, and decide now to engage adaptive strategies and keep moving forward—regardless of age or challenges. Use Ageless Thinking and Resilience to prevent age from defining who you are and what you're capable of in daily life, and in the face of adversity.

c. Functional Assets: Strength, mobility and endurance are mission-critical to lifelong vitality. The biggest roadblock to physical independence is blaming the loss of functional ability on age. Volumes of research prove that inactivity – not age – causes functional decline, yet people still often respond to decline by making their world smaller – giving up things they enjoy because they become more difficult.

Functional loss is usually gradual, easy to ignore. Immediate feedback would serve us better! If we didn't strength train, walk briskly, or practice balance and mobility for a week and couldn't get out of bed on day seven, cause and effect would sink in! It may take years to see the impact of chronic inactivity – but make no mistake – it's devastating. Stop squandering these valuable assets and commit to maximizing function!

Step 3: Make deposits

It's not enough to have a plan and identify vitality assets. You have to choose action and make deposits! Lifelong vitality isn't a choice you make once. It's dozens of choices you make every day about what you believe, how you spend your time, how much you move your body, what you eat, and how you face life's challenges. Compounded over time these small choices either support or sabotage your chances for lifelong vitality.

Don't leave your health to chance! Consciously examine your personal aging scripts then make a plan, balance your vitality assets, and make regular deposits for lifelong health. Create a personal *Vitality Portfolio*®!

About Kay

Kay Van Norman, President of Brilliant aging is an internationally-acclaimed thought leader in healthy aging as a speaker, author, and consultant. Her passion is uncovering hidden barriers to aging well and motivating action! Knowing what to do really isn't the problem – it's the gap between knowing and doing. Kay created the *Vitality Portfolio®* approach as a simple pathway to action – one that helps people embrace life and ignite joy – regardless of age or challenges.

Kay started out teaching dance and co-directing the Montana State University Dance Company. She also directed MSU's *Young at Heart* exercise program for older adults and was fascinated – by both the people, ages 50 to 90, and the perfect demonstration of how daily choices *compounded over time* impact lives.

She dove into the world of healthy aging, creating award-winning wellness products and writing two books, several book chapters, and scores of journal articles on aging well. Kay is known for her innovative approach to activating wellness – one that integrates research from multiple disciplines – whole person wellness, resilience, behavior change, exercise, and the mind/body connection to lifelong health. Her super-power is helping people peel back layers of attitudes and expectations to figure out which *aging scripts* are driving health choices.

The wellness industry took notice! Kay directed the Keiser Institute on Aging, and has worked with a wide range of companies – from GE Healthcare, NuStep, and Brookdale Senior Living, to the International Council on Active Aging, and Thailand's Ministry of Health – to name a few. Her international influence also includes a Chinese translation of her second book, *Exercise and Wellness for Older Adults*, and a chapter on ageism for the World Economic Forum book, *Global Ageing – Peril or Promise*.

Kay's business IS **lifelong vitality**, and *doing well while doing good* isn't just a catch phrase. She's a subject matter expert for consumer advocacy groups *Sixty & Me* – a community of over half-a-million members around the world, and the *Growing Bolder Media Group*, who on average reach 20 million people per week. Her mission is to change the way people view and experience aging by revealing barriers, activating strategies, and mobilizing businesses to empower customers.

The worldwide need to activate healthy aging has never been greater, which means the opportunity to build relationships with the largest consumer majority on the planet is also unparalleled! Kay recently created a series of healthy aging videos designed to engage leads and build relationships on client websites. With a unique Montana backdrop, they've been described as – *inspiring healthy aging in a way that feels like chatting on the porch with a friend.*

Kay lives with her family and three horses in Bozeman, Montana. She performs with a local dance company, explores the glorious Montana mountains all summer on horseback, and loves spending time with her kids and grandkids.

Would you like to elevate your brand with Boomers and beyond, inspire audiences, activate healthy aging in your community, or ignite personal vitality?

Contact Kay at:

- www.kayvannorman.com
- Email: kayvn@kayvannorman.com

CHAPTER 11

NEVER GIVE UP

BY ARI BERNSTEIN, M.D.

The huge house on the water, the fancy sports cars, the trips to exotic locations, people see the outcome of all the struggle, but they don't see the blood, sweat, and endless tears…the long days and nights…the years of struggling over money…the pain and suffering…the fights with the spouse or partner and near divorces. Success isn't overnight, although to many, it appears that is how it was achieved. I have to admit, I always knew deep down inside I would be successful and do whatever it took to make it, although, I had no clue what I was getting myself into. I don't think many do when they set out on the path to their dreams, although the ones who are willing to do whatever it takes to accomplish their goals seem to break any barrier in their path, and nothing is ever able to stop them from finding success.

Growing up without a father, since my parents were divorced when I was only six months old, seemed to put me at a disadvantage early in life, at least according to others. That isn't the way I saw it. I had my goals at an early age, and wasn't afraid to let people know them. I was always told what I couldn't do. Endless numbers of people told me I would never be a doctor for various reasons, from the subtle hints to straight to my face. Boy, did it feel good when I walked across the stage at my medical school graduation. I have to say a part of me chose to go to medical school just to prove to myself that I could do it, and to prove all those people wrong. I was on an endless mission and nothing would get in my way or stop me until I made it. Then the day came when I was finally a practicing physician, and I said to myself, 'well, I made it, what's next?' I think this is what sets apart successful people from the average. Successful people are always looking for 'what's next?'

I remember the day, like it was yesterday, I came home from a night shift from the hospital and got out of my brand new BMW. I just bought a new boat, I had fixed up my house I had purchased three years back, and I thought to myself, I finally made it. All my dreams are going to come true. I knew it was time to plan my next big move. Little did I know what life had in store for me that would change me forever. It was July 2011, and I started having back pain. Like most doctors, why would we need to go to the doctor, right? Big mistake. I opened my eyes one Sunday morning after playing cards with my friends late at night and I could not stand up. My whole right leg was totally numb and was in extreme back pain. I ended up having surgery on my back a few weeks later but never got better. I needed a cane to hobble around and was in the worst pain in my life.

In January 2012, I had my second surgery. I was told I had a large ruptured disc that was still ruptured and a tear in my spinal nerve and I would need a spinal cord stimulator placed. I was told, I would be lucky if I walked normally again, and most likely working as a physician again was near impossible. As you can imagine, I was crushed. I was in complete denial. I was depressed, didn't want to live anymore, and for over a year this just went on where I laid on the couch daily. I was in too much pain to do anything else. I couldn't even play with or hold my young children. It seemed to me, my life was over, I had given up.

You learn a lot about yourself, when you have over a year to lay on the couch and do absolutely nothing and it's only you and your thoughts. See, the problem was, my thoughts were controlling me, and they were controlling my attitude, my feelings, my actions and my eventual outcome. At the time, I didn't even realize this. I did realize that if I ever got better I would make an impact. I promised myself I would do something special with my life. Having a degree in psychology, I decided if I could learn to control my thoughts, maybe my outcome would be different. Maybe all those doctors were wrong. Maybe I could heal myself. Maybe I will be successful more than I ever imagined.

This is when I became aware of The Secret. The Law of Attraction. It is truly amazing what one can accomplish just with their own thoughts. The Law of Attraction states that whatever is coming into your life you are attracting into your life. Well, wait, did I attract my back injury? Well, maybe I did, because if I did not, I would not have ever learned the Law of Attraction and I would not be writing this chapter in this book right now. If you learn to think positive thoughts, you then start to feel positive feelings, and in turn this will change your behavior to more positive behavior. I quickly went from laying on the couch thinking my life is over, to seeing the right doctors and people who can get me better, going to rehab 3-4 days a week, doing rehab seven days a week at home, going to whole-body cryotherapy 3-4 days a week and getting my spinal cord stimulator. After a fourth back surgery, a spinal fusion about one year later, I was walking normally again and I was eventually back at work. Not only back at work, but working as an emergency room physician in one of the busiest ER's in the country.

Success is not as complicated as it seems. It can be very overwhelming at first when you have a big dream, but it's the little things that determine how far you will go. When you change your thoughts, you change your life. It may sound obscure, but the path is quite easy to explain. When you think positive thoughts, you start to feel positive feelings. This creates behavior changes that you may not even realize at first. These behavior changes attract people and situations into your life which lead you in the path towards your success. It's amazing how with just a simple mind shift, I started to see people and circumstances show up into my life that I needed, and I had no explanation for it. It just happened.

Many people learn the Law of Attraction, and still they just can't seem to figure it out. That is exactly why it's not working. There is nothing to figure out. If you are trying to figure out the Law of Attraction and how to be successful you are already on the wrong path. If you are trying to figure it out that means you don't have the belief that you are already on the right path. The first step in success is believing that you will accomplish it. There cannot be a plan B, there cannot be any if's and's or buts, it has to be an unwavering belief that you will make it happen. When I learned the Law of Attraction and I was lying on the couch with my back injury, I made a decision. I told myself, either I was going to get completely better, walk normal, have no pain, and achieve all my dreams, or I was going to die trying. There was nothing in between. Then I got to work. Are you willing to do anything to be successful?

Most medical doctors think the mind and the body aren't connected, and you cannot heal the body with the mind. This is so far from the truth. If I did not just prove that to you above, I don't know what else will. The problem lies in not conceptualizing how the mind can heal the body, but it is really quite simple. If your thoughts (mind), are positive, you will take the required actions to get the help, treatment, or whatever it takes to get better or heal yourself. The thoughts (mind), create behavior change that causes the body and the health of the body to improve indirectly—not directly. No one is sitting there thinking they are going to get better and they just get better, this is not how it works. It is from a behavior change caused by your thoughts (mind). This is no different than what it takes to be successful in anything in life. It all starts with belief. You need to believe in order to achieve.

I believe certain subconscious thoughts from my childhood led to my back injury which furthers my interest in the Law of

Attraction. This is a harder one to explain, but it is explainable. You see, when people are under stress, they get muscle spasms, most notably at night during sleep during the unconscious thought. This could lead to muscle spasm and pressure on a spinal disc, which over time could definitely cause a spinal disc to herniate and rupture. I know for some it's hard to believe they attract not only the good into their life, but also the bad. This is why learning to master the Law of Attraction and the power of your thoughts is the single most important factor that will determine your success.

Growing up without a father, having four back surgeries with a spinal cord stimulator placed, and being told I may never work again and/or possibly never walk normal again, never stopped me from seeing my vision through. Behind every successful person there are stories of suffering, pain and heartache. It is how you train your mind to handle these that determines how far one can go. Learning the Law of Attraction and how it helped me overcome these obstacles has led me on a lifelong path of learning and growth. In order to be successful, you first need to have a burning desire to achieve your dreams. With unwavering desire, and positive thought, anyone can manifest anything they want or need into their life. I have learned that the single most important factor on the journey to success is, no matter what gets in your way, no matter what obstacle you have to overcome, no matter who says that you will never succeed, you never give up!

About Ari

Ari Bernstein, M.D. grew up on Long Island, New York and went to Syosset High School. His interests in medicine and science led him as a young child to programs at Cold Spring Harbor Laboratory and science summer camp. He eventually went on to study pre-med and psychology at Long Island University CW Post. During college, he spent a summer back at Cold Spring Harbor labs learning and assisting with the Human Genome Project. He furthered his research interest when he spent time assisting a post-doctoral fellow at Columbia University College of Physicians and Surgeons during his college years.

Dr. Bernstein went on to graduate magna cum laude, and had a 3.9 GPA within his psychology major. Ari completed his medical school at St. George's University School of Medicine, his Internal Medicine residency at New York Presbyterian-Queens, and is Board-certified in Internal Medicine.

His strong interest in entrepreneurship and the improvement of the current healthcare system led him to invest and join the medical advisory board of Fruitstreet Health, a telemedicine diabetes prevention program startup.

Ari's medical experience includes internal medicine, emergency medicine and working with various healthcare administrations. He has a strong interest in leading healthcare teams to deliver outstanding patient care.

Ari has spent extensive time studying self-development and the Law of Attraction, and prides himself on helping others learn and grow. His future interests include business, real estate and the use of his knowledge and experience to make an impact on the lives of others.

His interests outside of medicine include sports, fishing, animals, marine aquariums, helping various charity medical organizations fight cancer and disease, and spending time with his family and pets.

You can connect with Ari at:

- www.linkedin.com/in/arisbernstein
- www.twitter.com/AriBernsteinMD
- www.AriBernsteinMD.com

CHAPTER 12

YOU ONLY GET WHAT YOU ORDER™

BY ANN MARIE SMITH

I'll never forget the first time I watched *The Secret* movie and heard author Jack Canfield share his wisdom on the law of attraction. It was the Spring of 2006, and in a darkened theater I sat riveted, captivated by his smile while clutching to each word of advice spoken. Then something he said struck me. It was such a powerful statement that from that day forward it became my personal mantra – even though it was the farthest thing from reality.

Repeated daily were my version of his words: *"I live in a four-and-a-half-million-dollar mansion, I have a husband to die for, we have the most amazing kids, I get to vacation in all the fabulous spots of the world."* I know my friends and family thought I had completely lost my mind. Here I was, saying this daily with such belief and conviction when I didn't even have two nickels to rub together!

So let me go back in time a little. I have always been a spiritual person. Even as a child, I loved talking to God. Along with my daily spiritual conversations, I made it a habit to practice principles gathered from the numerous books devoured on the power of intention and goal setting.

It was 1998, I was broke and stumbling from a failed marriage and realized that I would have to do something dramatically different if I wanted a better life. I wasn't even at the point of wishing for a dream life, just a better life. I had goals: I wanted to be wealthy. I wanted to make a difference in this world, and I wanted a gorgeous, sweet, smart husband and remarkable children. Pretty simple, I thought, right? How was I going to go from where I was to where I wanted to be? The first step was to reboot my life. With nerves and excitement, I took the leap to go back to college to get my degree in education and spent time *nourishing my mind.*

One night, I was feeling pretty down. It seemed that I was surrounded by people who were successful, both in their careers and in love. You know the kind of couples who hold hands, gaze deeply into each other's eyes and then break out into endless giggles. It was a bad night, or so I thought. I decided to show everyone (like anyone even noticed), that I was so happy and that I wasn't one bit bothered at their wealth, romantic lives, beauty, etc.

Stepping into my local Barnes & Noble, I headed straight for the self-help section. The first book that popped out at me was *The Aladdin Factor* by Jack Canfield. I sat on the floor and started to read. Once again, his words made an impact on me. I simply could not put the book down. I soon felt a tap on my shoulder as a nice lady said, "We are getting ready to close, but I can hold the book and you can come back tomorrow and finish reading it." I replied, "Thank you so much! I don't have any money today, but I am going to be extraordinarily wealthy one day and I promise that I will always buy books from you." She smiled, and we parted ways. Like clockwork, after a full day of work and school, I returned the next day to finish reading *The Aladdin Factor.*

Oh my goodness! What I learned was amazing and began to change my life in a good and scary way. You see, I had to re-define my belief system, and while in the midst of sitting at

Barnes & Noble – I had my epiphany. I had to order my life. I had to order exactly what I wanted. But first, what did I want? What *exactly* did I want?

I learned in *The Aladdin Factor* that there are barriers to asking for what you want. Here are the ones that spoke to me:

- Not knowing that you can ask, the correct way to ask, or even know what you really want.
- Growing up, societal expectation (parents, school, and especially media) teach us that it is inappropriate to ask for anything, we should be content with what we have, and that we shouldn't be a burden on others.
- Fear of being made to look stupid or humiliated if the request is rejected, fear of being cast aside for being too 'needy.'
- A majority of people have self-esteem issues, don't feel like their needs are important, and are happy to get anything at all, even if it's not what they want.

I kept thinking about this and it quickly hit me: I could order with faith and determination! I strode to the local taco shop. I placed my order…*exactly like I wanted it.* I never doubted that I would get what I ordered. I never "got stuck" on where the beans came from, how fresh was the guacamole or if they would get my order right. I ordered it and I got it. I focused on what I wanted, believed that I would get it and I did. This lesson shook me to the core and stuck with me every single time I ordered something, I got it. *So wait a minute, what if I used this strategy in my life?*

I was eager to use my newfound knowledge and test my theory. I began by "ordering" myself a full-time teaching job that paid $65,000 a year. I placed my order for a beautiful house in an exclusive neighborhood and I flipped through my personal catalog to order myself a husband – who was tall, athletic and smart. In my garage, I put up what I called a Vision Board— where I placed a picture of me in a classroom teaching as well as a picture of John F. Kennedy Jr. (I figured if I was ordering, I would order big!) I noted the exact date I expected them to show up, but on July 16, 1999 JFK Jr. was killed. I was crushed, but I knew without any doubt, that the person who was right for me, and who I had ordered, was out there.

Fast forward to 2001, the year I chose where the three things I ordered would show up. I had such a strong belief that I would get what I ordered. No doubt in my mind at all. Remember, I have faith! I earned a full-time job that paid $80,000 a year, bought a 3,400-square foot home on my dream street and my future husband came into my life.

By 2003, I decided to be even more intentional in my ordering. My husband (yes, he resembles JFK Jr.!), was told he couldn't have children, and twice in his previous marriage had adopted. My husband too was adopted and came from a family where all four children were adopted, this was a huge moment – I decided that I would like to order a daughter. I wanted my husband, who is just one of the most amazing men I know, to experience his qualities in a child of his own. I proceeded to find the cutest picture of a baby girl and put her on my vision board. My husband saw the new picture, and reminded me that it might not happen. I just smiled.

In August of 2003, we were blessed with the news that I was indeed pregnant. I had been carrying our child and didn't know it. January 2004 quickly came and our beautiful daughter, Kaitlyn, was born. As soon as we got home from the hospital, I found a picture of a baby boy, and yes, placed it on my vision board. Why waste time, I figured? While Kaitlyn is just three months old, we are amazed to find out that I'm pregnant, again! The new year of 2005 brings our son, Michael, into the world. These incredible events have made a huge impact on our lives and the power of ordering what you want is very surreal in our home. My husband is now a true believer in ordering!

Wanting to align my goals and dream even bigger, I once again used Jack Canfield as a touchstone. I ordered his book *The Success*

Principles: How to Get From Where You Are to Where You Want to Be and knew that he had written that book for me. I quickly became immersed in practicing the principles and applying them in my life. I went from one vision board to four with an exclusive board that I call "Dreams Accomplished." In case I start to doubt, this is a powerful reminder that what I order I get. Since reading Success Principles, I have ordered rental properties and companies. I own homes and cars, take vacations, develop deeper relationships, and have applied it to even the simplest things like a front row parking spot at Target. *When I am focused on what I want, I always get what I order.*

American entrepreneur and bestselling author Tony Robbins said, "Success leaves clues. Go figure out what someone who was successful did, and model it. Improve it, but learn their steps. They have knowledge." So remember all the hours I spent reading at Barnes and Noble? I was looking for the clues, the success blueprint. I read about people who had achieved the level of success I wanted, and then as Brian Tracy said, "find out what other successful people are doing, and then do the same things, over and over." This is what I did:

- Identify what I want – e.g., when you go to a restaurant, what do you want to eat?
- Order what you want – write it down and be specific – e.g., I want a husband like JFK Jr or better.
- Find a picture to match what you ordered – Yes I had a picture of JFK Jr.
- Put your pictures in a place where you will see them several times a day—I use a cork board and place one in my garage, office and bathroom.
- Believe—this is big. You have to believe that you deserve what you order and that you will get it.
- Act as if—Jack Canfield said, "Act as if you already have it."
- Be grateful for everything you already have, take care of what you have; you can't get more if you don't appreciate what you already have.

The art of ordering is a big deal for our family. Every day after Thanksgiving, my husband and I place our individual orders for the next year. We review our previous year's orders and look at how we did. We make new individual goals as well as joint goals for our family that include family vacation times, spiritual things and family health goals. We review and gather input from the kids on our family order and once we are all in agreement, they are posted on the family vision board.

This year, I wanted to meet Jack Canfield personally and co-author a book with him. On my vision board, I placed my order with a captured picture of Jack with Oprah. I glued my face over Oprah's. (When I meet her, also on my board, I will apologize.) In October 2017, I spent four full days at the Jack Canfield Luxury retreat. To say the experience was priceless would be an understatement. I had the opportunity to work with Jack Canfield and Patty Aubery and their amazing team. I tried really hard not to look or act like a groupie. But to sit by Jack and Patty and learn from them, I couldn't help but pinch myself to make sure I wasn't dreaming. Oh, and my order to co-author a book? Well, the fact that you are reading this is just a glimpse. My order has now grown, and you will have to wait and see what I get.

I can't overemphasize how powerful our minds are. We owe it to ourselves to read every book that nourishes our minds, reach for new opportunities and ways to continue our development to our full potential. My why is as Oprah Winfrey, who doesn't know she is my best mentor, said, "What material success does is provide you with the ability to concentrate on other things that really matter. And that is being able to make a difference, not only in your own life but in other people's lives."

It's a gorgeous day in beautiful, sunny, Southern California. I'm watching my dogs run playfully in the backyard of my home. As I watch them, I can't help but get teary-eyed with gratitude. You see, I now live in a multi-million-dollar home, have a husband to die for, have the most amazing kids, and travel to the most fabulous places in the world.

And what of my promise to Barnes and Noble? You bet – I buy hundreds of books from them a year. I will be forever grateful to Jack Canfield and all the authors who taught me that:

You Only Get What You Order.

About Ann Marie

Passionate about creating a life of her dreams, Ann Marie Smith has spent years researching the blueprints of success. She knew there was more to life than just existing. She knew that with the right tools, she could learn to intentionally create a life that would matter and make a difference in the world, and with an abundance of financial resources, she could serve the needs of others as well as her own.

Ann Marie Smith is a 35-year-veteran educator and entrepreneur. In 2009, she resigned her position as a school administrator to pursue her dream of becoming an entrepreneur. She is the CEO of 15 companies with over 600 employees. After spending over two decades working as a teacher and administrator, developing educational programs for her community, she learned what truly drives people and how to bring out the best in her teams. She has mastered how to connect with people in a way that brings out the best in them and teaches them how to become servant leaders that bring out the best in their teams.

Ann Marie is an award-wining professional and entrepreneur. She has landed coverage in print and broadcast outlets around the world, including the Univision, Telemundo, CBS, NBC, ABC, iheart radio and most recently *Success Today*. In addition to her extensive background in education and business, she most recently earned her California Contractors License, to pursue her goal of building custom homes for at-risk members of her community. Ann Marie holds a master's degree in Human Development/ Educational Leadership and Social Change.

Ann Marie leverages positive psychology to assist people to focus on their best qualities and talents and then uses that to help them develop into amazing leaders. She is passionate about creating jobs for people and growing them to become leaders in her companies.

Ann Marie lives in Southern California with her husband and two children. In her spare time, she loves investing in real estate, reading, going to the movies, watching her six dogs and micro-pig play, listening to music, and just laughing and having fun with her friends and family. Asked what she believes is the key to her success: Meditation, prayer, gratitude, giving to others, and making everything she does fun … if it isn't fun, she's not doing it.

If you would like to learn more about the techniques Ann Marie uses or for information on upcoming books, contact Ann Marie at:

- www.crazyamazingme.com.

CHAPTER 13

BETTER BY TONIGHT™: THE CEO'S GUIDE TO WINNING AT HOME LIKE YOU WIN AT WORK

BY NANCY HAMILTON

You can't go back and change the beginning, but you can start where you are and change the ending.
~ C. S. Lewis

People tell me everything. I have come to expect this over the last twenty years as a therapist and now executive coach. Yet, for as long as I can remember, perfect strangers...at the gym, store, even at the DMV... have wanted to tell me their life story.

My family just rolls their eyes, and I can't really blame them. Once we almost missed our flight for a family vacation when the ticket agent at the airport began telling me about her mom's move to assisted living. Believe me, I just wanted to know if I could get an aisle seat. Somehow, and much to the dismay of my family and the people in the line growing behind me, the ticket agent chose that moment to fill me in.

So not long ago, it was no surprise when the man sitting next to me at a conference began telling me his life story. Over the next two days "Michael" (not his real name), told me about his work, health, and marriage. He was a top achiever and the CEO of a tech company that just made the Fortune 50 list. Like so many successful executives, Michael had neglected himself and his relationships in the process.

He was overweight, in poor health and had just returned to work after having heart bypass surgery. He also said that for the past six years, he and his wife of 31 years had been in a sexless marriage. I guess I shouldn't have been shocked by this (given the tell-me-everything tattoo on my forehead), but I'll have to admit I was a little taken aback.

"You're not trying to pick me up are you?" I asked.

"Heavens no," he said.

"Whew!" I said. "Do you want to know what I think?"

"Please," he said, without hesitating.

"As someone who coaches executives or as a woman?"

"Both," he said, sipping his coffee.

"Well," I said, eyeing him more closely. "I know I hardly know you, but I wonder if you've ever considered that you might be the problem?"

Michael choked on his coffee, "You mean the fact that I had an affair?"

"Well yes, but it's more than that."

He went on to say, "I've tried everything to make it up to her. Counseling, Caribbean cruises and of course eating a whole bunch of crow. She still wants nothing to do with me."

Clearly, Michael had the "guilt and apology" thing down pat. What he didn't understand, however, was that infidelity is just a *symptom* of a larger issue. Unfortunately, neither a steady diet of crow nor "Romance of the Sea" cruises would cut it when it came to making things right with his wife.

I wanted to challenge him to look at himself because *self-awareness* is the first step to fixing any problem. Unless he started there, the sexless doghouse was likely where Michael would stay.

Incidentally, I want you to know that even though I'm pretty good at sizing up a situation, I don't make it a habit of telling perfect strangers what I think...at least not without their permission. The reason I'm telling you about Michael is in case some of you may also be "professionally making it but personally faltering." Maybe you're not a heart attack waiting to happen, or in a sexless marriage or even having an affair (yet). With the exception of never enough time and not enough sex, you may even think things at home are fine.

But if you're like a lot of executives in your position, your love life is not firing on all cylinders and, let's face it, you're tired of not getting what you want.

If this is the case, I'd like to ask you a few questions:

1. When you press the garage door opener at the end of the day do you ever think, "I can't even remember when my spouse and I took the time for a conversation of any substance... let alone the last time we had sex?"
2. Do you feel guilty about being away from your family and at the same time, pissed that you're not getting your needs met when you *are* home?

3. Do you spend so much of your time at the office because it's one of the few places where you feel appreciated, seen and respected?

If you answered yes to any of these questions, you're not alone.

The growing chasm between the accomplishment, admiration and respect executives experience at work, and the loneliness, isolation, and invisibility they feel at home has a lot to do with why so many successful men aren't winning at home like they win at work.

Some life coaches would approach the place you're in as a work-life "balance" issue. But you and I both know that if better time management, more vacations with your spouse, a personal trainer and avocado toast for breakfast resulted in having the love and sex you wanted, you wouldn't need their help or mine.

In my view, the disconnect between your professional and personal success boils down to two things: *self-awareness* and something I call *"Relationship Fluency."*

By self-awareness, I mean the ability to:

1. Recognize your emotions and their effect on others.
2. Know your strengths and limits.
3. Possess a strong sense of self-worth and your capabilities.

Once you have this kind of self-awareness, you are poised to learn the other half: Relationship Fluency. Relationship Fluency (RF) is a method that I developed over the past twenty years working with executives and their significant others.

I define RF as *the ease with which we relate to others.* Think of this "ease" as the understanding and communication that just flows when you are fluent in a language. RF works to improve all relationships, not just with your spouse. Your kids, parents, friends, and colleagues can all benefit.

RF makes any relationship, whether you're in a love relationship or not, feel just right...kind of like hitting the sweet spot on a tennis racquet or golf club; it's the royal road to having the relationship you want.

Now that you know a little bit about what RF is and what it should feel like, let's look at the three legs of the Relationship Fluency stool:

1. **A**ccessibility
2. **R**esponsiveness
3. **E**ngagement.

You can remember this by the acronym "A.R.E.", which is a method developed by Dr. Sue Johnson, and is the basis of the Hamilton Relationship Fluency A.W.A.R.E. Scale. Read on to learn more about each of these qualities:

Accessibility is not only about being reachable by phone, text or email, although these can be great ways to stay connected and show your partner that you're thinking of them. *RF Accessibility* has to do with how easy it is for your partner to get your *undivided* attention and how well you *listen* once he/she has it.

Responsiveness is when you and your partner rely upon each other and respond in both good situations and bad at an *emotional* level. For instance, whether your partner aced that presentation to the board or totally bombed it, your ability to tune in and respond with empathy and kindness is key. *RF Responsiveness* gives the message that you and your partner are not alone in the world and that you have each other's back.

Engagement happens when you are mutually attracted to each other, and you want to be involved with each other physically, emotionally, and intellectually. When you and your partner have *RF Engagement*, you both feel noticed, physically desired, intellectually stimulated and valued in every way.

Why don't we start by seeing how much of each of these you already have by taking the little test below? Now that you have a better idea of what A.R.E. is all about, use your best guess as to how your partner sees these qualities in you. The good news is you don't even have to *agree* with your significant other's point of view. By viewing it through your partner's eyes, you will automatically increase your self-awareness (remember how important that is) and start to build another important skill: the ability to put yourself in your partner's shoes.

In other words, A.R.E. you Relationship Fluent? A.R.E. you ready to become Relationship Fluent? You can start by using my **Better by Tonight**™ tips:

Better by Tonight™ Tips for Increasing Accessibility:

1. Respond to your partner's communication (text, call, email, smoke signal) as quickly as possible, even if it's just to say, "I can't talk now, but I'll call you as soon as I can."
2. When you do see each other again, give your partner at least 20 minutes of uninterrupted and undistracted time to debrief the day. Put away all phones, computers and anything that could distract you from giving undivided attention.
3. Maintain eye contact with your partner and ask questions like, "What was the best part of your day and why?"
4. Try asking "permission" before bringing up anything potentially controversial. Say something like, "I have some ideas about what we talked about. Is now a good time to share them?" is respectful and gives your partner the option of saying, "Sure, honey, lay it on me." or "I'm so hungry I could eat my arm. Let's talk after dinner."

Better by Tonight™ Tip for Increasing Responsiveness:

1. Try responding to your partner's news, whether good or bad by using the Harville Hendrix active listening technique of <u>mirror</u>, which lets your partner know that you can see how he/she is responding to any given situation, <u>validate</u> which

lets your partner know why it makes perfect sense that he/she feels the way they do. (Note: you do not need to agree with them to be able to see it from their perspective). The third step is to <u>empathize</u> with your partner by guessing what he/she might be feeling (happy, sad, glad, hurt, scared, etc.).

<u>Example:</u> Here's an example of how *Mirror, Validate* and *Empathize* work:

- Your board meeting took longer than expected, and your wife is upset that you were late for dinner once again. Say, "I can see that you are upset that I am late." – (Mirror)
- "That makes perfect sense. I know that our family dinners are important to you because you want our family to have time together." – (Validate)
- "And when I'm not here on time I am guessing that you feel unimportant and like you and the kids aren't a priority for me." – (Empathize)

Better by Tonight™ Tips for Increasing Engagement:

Increase your partner's ability to trust and confide in you by saying things like, "Help me understand." and "What can I do to help?" When you communicate like this consistently, it sends a message to your partner that you are a "safe place to land." Over time, this will likely lead to your partner softening and wanting you to come closer emotionally and physically.

1. Know your partner's love language by having him/her take the 5 Love Languages test. This is a fantastic tool from Gary Chapman that both of you should run-don't-walk to take. Once you learn your partner's primary love language, whether it's primarily Gifts, Words of Affirmation, Quality Time, Acts of Service or Physical Touch, you will thank Gary, your lucky stars and me. (www.5lovelanguagestest.com).

2. Use the 3-Part Apology. You've probably noticed how well it goes over when you say something like, "I'm sorry you had

a problem with that." or when your kids say, "sorEEEE!" accompanied by an eye roll. Owning how we hurt others and making amends is one of the best ways to enhance **RF Engagement**. Here's what you say instead: "I'm sorry. I messed up. How can I make it up to you?" Then for goodness sakes, use *your partner's* love language to make it up to him/her.

SUMMARY

In summary, I realize I've given you a lot to think about. My hope is that with newfound awareness and a kickass tool like Relationship Fluency, your relationships will be easier, you will feel closer and have a better (and sexier) love life.

Take some time to reflect on what I've said. Go hit some golf balls. Thumb through a stack of Oprah magazines. Maybe even spend a minute being grateful that some sassy stranger hasn't asked you to take a good look at yourself. But whatever you do, just don't let this be "shelf help" and one more thing that you read and never use.

You may not be able to change the beginning, but by starting with you, I'm pretty confident you can change the ending.

About Nancy

Nancy Hamilton is founder and CEO of Hamilton Coaching Strategies. She is an executive coach for high-level executives who have attained great success professionally but personally they want more. More love. More sex. More connection.

With training in clinical social work and 24 years in the field, Nancy has parlayed her knowledge and experience from individual and couples therapist to executive coach and mentor.

Using her signature programs of Relationship Fluency and Better by Tonight™, Nancy has spent more than 35,000 hours teaching executives and their significant others the relationship skills necessary for getting the love and sex they want – so they can "crush it in the bedrooms like they crush it in the boardrooms."

She has appeared on The Dr. Phil Show, NBC Dateline and ABC Nightline. Nancy is a considered an industry expert and thought leader in the areas of Emotional Intelligence and The Impact of Success on Executives and Families.

In addition to co-authoring *The Success Formula* with Jack Canfield, her own book, *The F-ability Factor: The Surprising Relationship Tool for Crushing it in the Bedroom Like You Crush it in the Boardroom*, will be published in the fall of 2019.

Nancy holds a bachelor's degree in psychology and humanities from the University of Colorado, Boulder and a master's degree in social work from Smith College in Northampton, Massachusetts.

A Colorado native, Nancy is a devoted hockey mom, dog lover and college basketball fan. She lives with her family in Westminster, Colorado.

Nancy is available for corporate consultations, one-on-one executive coaching, keynote speaking engagements and workshops.

Are you ready to become Relationship Fluent? Start by taking the A.W.A.R.E.

assessment at: www.hamiltoncoachingstrategies.com.

To contact Nancy:

- www.advancedexecutivedevelopment.com
- nancy@advancedexecutivedevelopment.com

CHAPTER 14

TAX-FREE RETIREMENT BEYOND THE ROTH IRA

BY STEVEN L. CRAWFORD, MBA, CFF®,
"The Retirement Wealth Coach®"

Many of us have heard all of the secrets and lessons "Mamas" have taught us for many years. For example, "always look both ways before crossing the street" or "don't touch the stove because it's hot!" Well, Mamas always have known best and I can surely appreciate some of the lessons I've learned from my "mama." One of the things I remember about my "mama" is her reading all of those childhood stories like *Bambi, The Cat in the Hat*, and this one in particular, *Cinderella.*

We all can remember the story where Cinderella was mistreated by her stepmother and stepsisters and made to do all of the menial chores, while her stepsisters were allowed to prepare for the ball in hopes of meeting the handsome prince. If you can recall, Cinderella's fairy godmother granted her the wish which eventually allowed her to attend the ball, but she had to leave before midnight after which everything would return to normal. Eventually, as we learn, Cinderella loses her slipper which led to the Prince searching for the owner of the glass slipper. That led to a mass proclamation to find who would fit this slipper that was worn by Cinderella.

Obviously, as the story unfolded, the glass slipper was fitted by Cinderella and she lived happily ever after with her prince charming. Now, why is Steve talking about Cinderella and a glass slipper? The answer is because too many famous financial experts have made blanket statements suggesting that everyone should never do this or do that. You've heard it many times I'm sure – "Buy Term, invest the difference." and "You shouldn't buy annuities because their fees are too high." but they never tell you that there are no-fee annuities and that all annuities are not the same, or that life insurance has more to offer than just a death benefit.

Essentially, what they are trying to do is make everyone wear the same proverbial glass slipper. You are "Cinderella" and your retirement planning is unique to you, so separating fact from fiction is extremely vital – which is what the goal is here. Now that we know you are "Cinderella," let's take a deeper look into various challenges that retirement will bring and why your retirement plans should include not only tax-deferred planning, but also tax-preferred planning – including Tax-Free options.

Most of us have heard by now about Roth IRAs and how they grow tax-free, but we need to understand how the Roth actually works and what its limitations are. The Roth is absolutely a beautiful, phenomenal vehicle. However, there are four limitations that you need to make sure you are aware of, and I wouldn't even go so far as to call them limitations as they are just guidelines. These are things that you need to know about the Roth – the four limitations or guidelines of the Roth:

(1) Income limit (You make too much money; the government does not allow you to put anything in).

(2) Contribution limit (This depends on how old you are – the most you can put in is either $6000 or $7000 if you are over the age of 50).

(3) 59½ rule. Are you familiar with the fact that if you try to take your money out, particularly your gains, you pay a 10% IRS penalty for accessing the money prior to reaching age 59½?

(4) Market Risk: What do you think your money is tied to as its investment options? Typically, it is tied to Mutual funds, which come with volatility. So, if it is tied to Mutual Funds, this means your principal is at risk. This doesn't make it a bad vehicle, but you just need to know the risks you are taking.

Also, keep in mind the 5-year rule regarding a Roth's tax-free status which states: Five years must have elapsed since the tax year of your first Roth contribution before the earnings can be withdrawn tax-free. That applies across the board to retirees, even if the account owner is 99 years old or a first-time homebuyer. Eligible Roth IRA contributors don't need to do anything special to ensure that only your contributions are withdrawn. The Roth goes by the rule, "first-in, first-out." That means that the money that went in first is the first to be distributed. You only need to worry about the 5-year rule if your withdrawal is in excess of the amount contributed and the IRS decrees that Roth IRA distributions are taken in this order:

1. Contributions.
2. Conversions or rollover contributions.
3. Earnings on investments.

What is the Five-Year Rule for Roth IRA Withdrawals?

Furthermore, an investor can withdraw his or her contributions to a Roth IRA at any time without tax or penalty. But that does not apply to any earnings or interest that you have earned on your Roth IRA investment according to IRS.gov. In order to withdraw your earnings from a Roth IRA tax and penalty-free, not only must you be over 59½ years-old, but your initial contributions must also have been made to your Roth IRA five years before the date when you start withdrawing funds. If you did not start contributing into your Roth IRA five years before your withdrawal, your earnings will not be considered a qualified distribution from your Roth IRA because the withdrawal violates the five-year rule.

This is also true for Inherited Roth IRAs that they can have a 5-year waiting period as well, but it starts with the original account owner. If the account owner dies before five years have elapsed, the clock keeps going when the inheritor gets it.

So, now that we've digested the Roth IRA, what are the other two tax-free vehicles that I can invest in? Well, one is Municipal Bonds. According to Investor.gov: Municipal bonds (or "munis" for short) are debt securities issued by states, cities, counties and other governmental entities to fund day-to-day obligations and to finance capital projects such as building schools, highways or sewer systems. By purchasing municipal bonds, you are in effect lending money to the bond issuer in exchange for a promise of regular interest payments, usually semi-annually, and the return of the original investment, or "principal."

A municipal bond's maturity date (the date when the issuer of the bond repays the principal) may be years in the future. Short-term bonds mature in one to three years, while long-term bonds won't mature for more than a decade.

Generally, the interest on municipal bonds is exempt from federal income tax. The interest may also be exempt from state and local taxes if you reside in the state where the bond is issued. Given the tax benefits, the interest rate for municipal bonds is usually lower than on taxable fixed-income securities such as corporate bonds.

The two most common types of municipal bonds are the following:

- General obligation bonds. These are issued by states, cities or counties and not secured by any assets. Instead, general obligation bonds are backed by the "full faith and credit" of the issuer, which has the power to tax residents to pay bondholders.
- Revenue bonds. Revenue Bonds are not backed by a government's taxing power but by revenues from a specific project or source, such as highway tolls or lease fees. Some

revenue bonds are "non-recourse", meaning that if the revenue stream dries up, the bondholders do not have a claim on the underlying revenue source.
(Information is courtesy of Investor.gov)

The challenges with Municipal Bonds are call, credit, interest, inflation, longevity and liquidity risks. In addition, and this is my opinion and shared by many advisors I know, that they are: low diversification, low yield, and unless you are a multi-millionaire looking for a small stream of income, there are better tax-free retirement options which leads me to the other tax-free retirement planning option: <u>Cash Value Life Insurance</u>. Yes, Life Insurance can be tax-free and does not have the 59½ rule of the Roth IRA nor does it have market risks associated with the Roth and Municipal Bonds.

Cash Value Life Insurance (CVLI) has been around a long time even going back to the time of JC Penny – who used his CVLI policy to fund his business during the depression and which allowed him to pay staff and succeed when the market was hemorrhaging. Not only JC Penny, but Ray Kroc (the one who started McDonald's), after convincing Maurice and Richard McDonald to sell him their hamburger stand and all of its trade secrets, took out a loan on two of his cash value policies to get McDonald's off the ground and well, you know the rest.

The fact that men like Ray Kroc and JC Penny knew the importance of not having all their eggs in one proverbial wealth "glass slipper," i.e., stocks and bonds offered via Wall Street, this is a lesson we all can learn from. In fact, most of my clients prefer CVLI for this very reason:

All those guidelines that applied to the Roth (market corrections, income limitations etc.) don't apply to CVLI. There is no income limit and no contribution limit for CVLI!

(Side note: Roth IRA is phased out but will go up by $2,000 for singles from $120,000 in 2018 to $122,000 in 2019. It will go up by $4,000 for married filing jointly from $189,000 in 2018 to $193,000 in 2019. You can't contribute anything directly to a Roth IRA when your income goes above $135,000 in 2018 and $137,000 in 2019 for singles, and $199,000 in 2018 and $203,000 in 2019 for married filing jointly, up by $2,000 and $4,000 respectively in 2019.)

So, putting those two together, the CVLI and the Roth IRA, as you start making more money, you can put more money in CVLI which is the reverse in a Roth. Because, as you make more money in a Roth, they phase you out! Also, there is no 59½ rule in life insurance because it is not an Erisa plan. Therefore, it is not subject to Erisa rules. You don't have a 10% penalty because of your age. And last but not least, you are 100% protected from market risk but can participate in a product called the Indexed Universal Life (IUL) which allows you to use an index like the S&P, but your money is never directly invested into the market. (At www.FigWealthAdvisors.com, we have uncapped strategies with participation above 100%, and in some cases, 200%.) Basically, you get all the gains with no risk to principal ever, and any gains cannot be lost due to future market volatility, they are locked in!

When the stock market corrects itself again (and it's never a question of *if*, only when), you won't lose a dime. Plus, you shift the responsibility from yourself to the insurance companies. Hey, isn't that the reason why we buy insurance, in case something happens. You have insurance on your car, home and even our cell phones, so let's insure your retirement.

The other reason why life insurance, in particular cash value life insurance, is important, is that America has $19 trillion in debt, and ironically, we have roughly the same in our 401(k)s and our traditional IRA accounts. So, logically, where do you think they are going to tax in order to make it up? Remember, those accounts are tax-deferred (have not been taxed yet), so the importance of tax-free planning beyond the Roth IRA with no limitations on income or contributions is akin to not trying to fit your retirement planning all into the glass slipper that many advisors have recommended.

The Success Formula for investing is understanding that a balanced portfolio consists of tax-deferred and tax-preferred retirement income planning.

About Steven

Steven L. Crawford, MBA, Certified Financial Fiduciary®, RFC®, National Social Security Advisor®, also known as The Retirement Wealth Coach®, is CEO and Managing Partner of FIG Wealth Advisors and Ford Insurance Group. He has 19 years' experience in the insurance and financial services industry, winning several awards working as a "Foundation Capital and Retirement Specialist." In addition, Mr. Crawford is a member of the National Association of Experts, Writers & Speakers®, National Ethics Association, National Black MBA Association and a Hall of Famer with a youth sports organization (Pembroke Pines Optimist) in Pembroke Pines, Florida.

Furthermore, Steve is a member of an exclusive group of only 3% of the nation's advisors who has specialized retirement products with two of the leading money management firms in the world just for his clients. He has extensive retirement income planning expertise with a focus on safe money and alternative non-correlated asset planning that secures retirement from stock market-related volatility that can erode life savings.

Mr. Crawford has been seen on CBS television show *Morning Break, CBS Local News at 5PM*, Fox Sports and NBC 6 South Florida. He is currently featured on the leading website in the world for "Safe Money" related searches. In addition, Steve is a financial instructor for a non-profit where he teaches retirement and safe money strategies for affluent attendees. Also, he is a sought-after advisor requested to teach estate preservation, retirement income for affluent attendees, and business continuation strategies for business owners at various businesses throughout the country.

Lastly, he is a former host to two ESPN Charlotte radio shows, *Preps 2 Pros with Steve Crawford* and *Coffee & Cash Flow* which aired for 3 years. Now, both shows have evolved into highly regarded Podcasts.

Steve's motto is: *To provide refined* <u>*Foundation Capital and Retirement Plan Solutions*</u> *primarily for a select group of individuals who, among other things, are looking to elevate the performance of their retirement assets, alleviate the concerns many have of "outliving your money," and aspire to a work-optional lifestyle.*

Mr. Crawford does this through a process he's developed and refined called TCE: TOTAL CLIENT ENGAGEMENT. This is a process of educating clients about what's really happening with your money in spite of the media or uncertainties of Washington and Wall Street.

CHAPTER 15

✓ACT ✓ACTING ✓ACTION ✓ACTIVITY ⇨ IMPACT✓✓✓

BY LYNDA FUSSELL

As a serial learner and 'early adopter', I found myself full of ideas and exciting new things I wanted to share with the world. But I kept on working really hard, long hours for my 'safe' backstop job while I tried to learn more or try out other new things that really interested me. The trouble was, I love learning and I'm naturally curious. But … I'm hugely competitive and at the same time, I didn't think I was ready. Or perhaps I didn't stop to question if 'I' was ready to make the changes I dreamed off.

It's a strange thing really. I've done it before, a few times … but in those days my girls were much younger and my parents independent. As my girls grew up and left home, I became more conscious of their views of me. The pedestal was high. I also had my parents to consider. They live with me and as they were aging, seemly small things were actually becoming really big things. I was aware that I could easily unnerve them with a passing comment about bills coming in and cash being limited – a not-uncommon scenario for a small business working with large corporates.

So, what changed? It's fair to say that the Universe was always backing me up and presenting very clear signposts and support, that I often ignored. I was doing ok, I had a part-time corporate consulting role, I loved my coaching clients and I was doing an increasing number of healing consultations whilst working on a couple of start-up businesses. Yeah, yeah. I had decided a few years earlier that I would never again be dependent on a single client for my income! So, I just worked harder, but always doing things I loved.

It all really hit home, in big multicolour neon lights, when I walked **The Camino Way** with a couple of friends. Ten days, 280 kilometres, 18 kilograms on my back, and temperatures in the upper 30's centigrade. I started to see, or really feel, the value of the many lessons and wise words that I had absorbed over the years. I was bursting with enthusiasm and the raw need to share my Lessons from The Camino.

With renewed vigour I took on more coaching clients and I was amazed at the extent and speed of the results. The lessons I'd learnt on my pilgrimage were deep, and personally meaningful. They flowed with such passion that I was able to convey my insights and understanding of personal hesitations and blockers. With gentle guidance and support, I watched client after client 'move mountains' and stride confidently into their vision.

And that was it. The penny dropped! There is so much guidance on finding your passion, creating your vision, establishing who your ideal client is and what they need.

But actually, so few people make it happen. I was one of those. I've had ideas – some good, some bad and some pretty amazing. I've watched other people bring my ideas to life, sometimes years after my business plan was written!

Frustrating… I just needed to take ACTION… to break down the invisible barriers and make it happen. My walk was a dream, that came to fruition after the death of a dear friend. Sometimes the

Universe deals us a really big dose of 'wake up'.

It has been life-changing for me, and for my clients.
I understand them...
I was there too...
I saw how the right support took their businesses...
and lives... to new heights...
I saw what I needed to do for me...
And today I live that...
I help others find their own inner strength and conviction...
Act don't React!

But...
Why is it so hard?
To make the leap from 'knowing' to 'doing'...
We read the books...
We attend the courses...
We listen avidly to experts...
We craft our visions...
We document our plans...

And...
We wait...
Wait for what?
Why?

There are many reasons, too many to mention here. The fascinating field of neuroscience is helping us, daily, to understand more about the inner-working of the mind. Studies on the effects of ancient practices are validating the 'known value' of meditation, chanting and mindful movements. We are human, and we are constantly evolving.

So, what have I learnt? And how does this influence my life now, my clients' lives, and yours, should you choose to take ACTION?

There are so many definitions of ACTION. Have you ever looked it up?

A few of my favourites that really emphasise why some people are so successful, and others are great dreamers, planners, strategists, [insert whatever applies here].

- The process of **doing something**, or **something done**, for a particular purpose, especially in order to deal with a problem or difficult situation, or achieving something.
- **Movement** – the way something moves or works, or the effect it has on something else.

ACTION has a number of related words that are all relevant to your success. Every entrepreneur needs to be very familiar, comfortable and engaged with many of them. It starts with the root, ACT.

TO ACT:

- To **behave** in the stated way
- To **do something** for a particular purpose or to solve a problem
- To **have an effect**
- **Perform**
- **Thing done** – something that you do
- **Performance**

These are amazing words and just about everything that you need to be successful. Just imagine that you have done your visualisation activity. W-o-o-o-w-w, there is that word again, ACTivity.

You have defined the WHY; you are aligned with your Purpose and your Passion. This is your reason to behave in The Way, to achieve something.

However, before you can make something 'come to life', you need to have a reason to start now. Without a compelling reason to Take ACTION / Create Movement there is no driver for you to Perform.

Are you beginning to see the theme?

With this understanding, I have created THE STEPS TO SUCCESS which is all about helping you TAKE ACTION.

Step 1: Define your initial plan.

> How you come up with an idea, be it through meditation, visualisation or singing in the shower, it will only ever be a thought unless you take Step 1 in the ACTION CYCLE.
>
> Thoughts become things is a well-known phenomenon. Too often, we only work with fear-based things. This is a natural human response – fight, flight or freeze!
>
> Focus instead on WHY you want to do this – the emotions that make you happy, taking into account your loves, strengths, hunches and gifts. Then, list out:
>
> - What is needed?
> - Who may help you?
> - When?
> - Where?
> - How?
>
> This is your initial plan. Brilliant! You have a plan. You have taken ACTION Step 1.
>
> This is a big step. Do this properly. Listen to your own instinct, your 'gut-feel'. 'Feel the Force', your force, your reason and driver for Why and Why Now.
>
> *Lessons from The Camino:*
>
> #LfTC1 **If you don't know where you are going you will have no idea when you have arrived.** We all wanted to do a long walk. Where should we go?

#LfTC2 **Once you have a destination, or end-goal defined, it is essential to establish where the starting point is.** You might know where you are heading but if you don't know where you are starting from how can you plan your journey and route?

Step 2: Start...

Get started. Do an ACTIVITY, any ACTIVITY, that takes you closer to your end-goal.

Use what you already know? Who can help you? Make that phone call. Do something, anything that is clearly aligned to, and required, to ACTION your plan.

If you are not quite sure what that might look like, pretend you know – get ACTING. Put on a performance that convinces you, and others, that you do know. In reality, if you have a heart-centred desire with a plan, you know what to do. ACT like it. Get the excuses out of your way and just start. ACT the person you want to be. Take on the role, right now. Get started today.

Even if you are working in another job, find a way to start. And follow the ACTION CYCLE.

Lessons from The Camino:

#LfTC3 **Once you know where you are headed it is essential to assess what you currently have and what you need for success.** Don't reinvent the wheel. Use what you already know, have or have access to.

#LfTC52 **You can do the journey regardless of your budget.** The way you do it may be different, but you can still do it!

Step 3: Be conscious of everything you do.

Make everything you do consciously in support of your goal, and if it isn't, know why it isn't. Take this mindful approach to everything in your day: every ACTION, every REACTION, every NO ACTION.

Every day do something. Do something for a particular purpose or to solve a problem. 'Take ACTION' is also defined as: begin working to make an idea or a plan happen or be successful.

Recently, while doing a jigsaw puzzle (yip, one of those real ones, not a computer generated one…), I was mindfully taking a break from a piece of work I was engaged with. I became aware that I was ACTIVELY targeting a certain colour or form and would scan over the beautifully laid-out pieces, picking up only those that resonated with the imprint I had of what was needed. I was consciously targeting colour shades and then piece shapes. Sometimes I did it the other way, shape first, then colour/pattern.

We do so much unconsciously, or sub-consciously, that our brain rules our life. The brain's primary function is to protect us. If you allow it, the brain will talk you out of anything. Become more conscious of everything you do, and you will bring your mind in control. Acknowledge the message from your brain, thank it for looking out for you, and then consciously, mindfully, make the decision, take ACTION that will move you closer to your goal.

Lessons from The Camino:

#LfTC31 **Keeping drinking water.** It is easy just to keep walking but without drinking enough water you will eventually get a headache, feel tired, or worse.

#LfTC15 **Know the end goal and just get going.** Book the flight. Gather the team. Set the dates. Schedule your leave. Do what it takes – just do something every day.

Step 4: Make mistakes. Lots of mistakes.

Make mistakes. Be disappointed. Be deflated. Only by trying things will you learn. Learn what works and what doesn't work. This might sound counter-intuitive. Scary even.

Without trying something new, something different, you will continue doing the same ol', same ol' – and nothing will change! Step outside your comfort zone. With movement, aka ACTION, you will establish the way something moves or works, or the effect it has on something else. And hey presto, you've learnt something new!

Lessons from The Camino:

#LfTC6 **When the going appears tough, keep going, break through your own barriers**. Setting yourself a big challenge and really pushing your boundaries is where the magic happens.

#LfTC8 **Early to bed, early to rise makes for a great day!** This was an interesting lesson for me. I used to like to work until everything was ready for the morning. Actually, you are far smarter after a good sleep!

Step 5: Reflect often. Take a moment. Gather your thoughts.

Whether things are working well, or not, take time to stop 'doing' and reflect. Do this at least once daily, ideally once an hour.

I have a timer clock on my laptop, that pings every 15 minutes. For 15 seconds, I yawn, I stretch, I flood my body with oxygen, I reset my amazing brain, I allow my mind to freewheel. Every hour I take 10 minutes to get up and walk away from my desk. By walking out of my office, I have a total break and return refreshed and ready to flow with renewed vigour.

You are able to get a fresh perspective on things by stepping away. You will become aware of something different to try, aware of the emotions, disappointment or excitement, that you have just experienced. Thoughts become things. Be sure that your thoughts are real, are really *Your Thoughts*, and not your brain trying to protect you.

Listen to your instinct. You know the answer. Trust yourself. Sleep on it. Sometimes after a night of dreaming, you awaken to the answer. Sometimes the 'shower moment' brings you the clarity. Be open to what you know deep inside. Be mindful and listen.

Lessons from The Camino:

#LfTC7   **Take time to reflect.** Absorb the feelings, learnings and experiences gained from the journey.

#LfTC32 **It's ok to take a break.** Listen to your body, the environment and the conditions.

Step 6: Keep going.

Always keep going. Take ACTION – ACT DON'T REACT.

When things are going well this is easy. Or is it? Sometimes we become complacent. ACT like the person you want to be. Keep that vision in focus. Apply your best ACTING skills and do something to achieve your objective. *Begin working to make an idea or a plan happen or be successful.* This may be another new product. Ask for support.

When you've had a set-back, perceived or real, KEEP GOING. Start again. Tweak. Redefine. Change direction. Do something. TAKE ACTION. Do something to deal with a particular task, problem or plan.

Lessons from The Camino:

#LfTC17 **Talk to others who have taken the journey.** They have words of wisdom to share.

#LfTC34 **Re-adjust the plan if necessary.** On a fiercely hot day, we stopped in the woods and slept for an hour.

Step 7: Measure. Monitor. Get feedback.

It is essential to regularly assess where you are going and how you are doing. Are you still aligned to your purpose? Are you still on track with your plan?

Constant monitoring and tracking, throughout the ACTION CYCLE, are essential ACTIVITIES to determine if you should continue with your current ACTIONS or if you need to try a new idea, or ACTION, to move you towards your goal.

Lessons from The Camino:

#LfTC44 **You get fitter, stronger, wiser the more you do something.**

These steps are a cycle and, as with life, create a steady flow of ACTIVITY. So often, I see amazing people with great ideas, who are passionate but fail to keep the ACTION CYCLE going, and therefore fail to realise their true potential. We owe it to ourselves, and to the source of our talents, to be the best we can be. You've done the visioning now take ACTION and create a truly magical IMPACT.

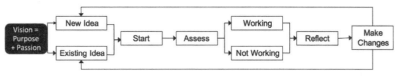

The Action Cycle – Act don't React!

#LfTC47 **So you want to do something different.** Without a reason to do something it either won't happen or, if it does, there is a real danger of dissatisfACTION or disappointment.

Without a plan you aren't going anywhere.

Take ACTION and begin working to make an idea or a plan happen and be successful.

About Lynda

Lynda Fussell is a coach and healer who works with clients all over the world. Individuals, small business owners and corporate teams all benefit from Lynda's support and guidance which is backed by years of coaching and mentoring.

Interspersed with the coaching activities, Lynda has continued to spend time doing corporate consultancy in the fields of change management, innovation and communications.

Lynda graduated with a Commerce Degree from the University of Natal, Pietermaritzburg, in South Africa. After a couple of years working in the Mining Industry in Johannesburg, Lynda found herself living on an Air Force Base near the Kruger Park. Her love of nature flourished as did her first business adventure, a horse-riding school. Here Lynda realised her talent for teaching, guiding teenagers through the tricky years of adolescence under the guise of horse riding, but ably assisted by some amazing equine facilitators.

Over the years, after living in a number of different countries and starting/ restarting various careers, Lynda has experienced different cultures, travelled widely, worked in massive corporates, small start-ups, and had a few private ventures too. Never one to sit idly, but always exploring the opportunities in encounters with the express aim of helping others to *be the best they can be.*

A few key life events have really shaped the way Lynda thinks, experiences life and people:

- A major accident in 2003 saw her on crutches and totally dependent on others for more than six months.
- She discovered Kundalini Yoga in late 2014, on a weekend retreat of raw food and yoga, and found a whole new level of meditation, exercise and relaxation. Lynda went on to join an online Academy and continues to practice most days.
- Formally qualifying as a Coach in 2015, after years of providing support to fellow colleagues in change projects – without realising that this was a profession called coaching!

- She made a walk along the Portuguese Coastal Camino Way with a couple of friends in 2017.
- In the following year, 2018, she provided the support vehicle for three amazing young cyclists riding from Land's End to John O'Groats – and raising money for two charities.

An avid reader, and follower, of inspiring people, Lynda is continually growing her understanding of how we humans work. The latest research in neuroscience, brain retraining, emotional distress, stress and trauma makes for a very deep complimentary repertoire to the business experience gained.

Writing has been a passion for many years and now it feels right to share some of her vast experience through this medium, complementing the consulting, coaching, mentoring, teaching and healing.

Lynda currently lives in the Spa Town of Harrogate, in North Yorkshire, England. She moved back to the UK in 2003 with her two girls, Patricia and Heather, who continue to be a major source of inspiration and pride.

Yorkshire provides the perfect backdrop for her retreats, walking and yoga getaways, and global coaching assignments.

You can contact Lynda at:

- lynda@lyndafussell.com
- www.lyndafussell.com/contact
- www.linkedin.com/in/lyndafussell
- www.facebook.com/LyndaMFussell
- www.twitter.com/lynda_fussell

CHAPTER 16

UNLOCK YOUR DREAMS

BY MARK & KATHRYN EASTHOPE

He who has Health has Hope. He who has Hope has everything.
~ Anonymous

Before I met my husband Mark, I was a single mom of five kids. I was experiencing some serious back problems, so bad that at one point I was stuck in bed for six weeks with a seized back. That was a stressful and challenging time. I was later diagnosed with Degenerative Disc Disease, and for a number of years, I had to live through an insurmountable amount of pain.

I became completely dependent on my family for help. I was living with my sister, her husband, their seven kids, and their dog, along with my five kids, all in one house...yikes! I couldn't do anything without somebody's help. I couldn't even roll over in bed because it was too painful.

Things started to change for the better when I married my sweetheart, Mark, in 2007. Incidentally, he also had five kids, so together we had ten children coming into the marriage. After our wedding, my back pain continued to come and go. It would seize up for a while, and I'd be stuck in bed for a couple of days, a week and sometimes a month or more. Eventually, it would let up, and I'd be able to do more 'normal' things again.

At first, the pain was intermittent. However, in time, it became significantly worse on a daily basis. I had to be very careful about what I did and did not do. For example, there were days when I would go out to weed the garden, and I would have to literally crawl back to the house in intense pain. Other days, I wouldn't even be able to crawl, and I would just have to lie there in the dirt in pain until Mark could come and carry me back into the house. He lovingly carried me up the stairs to our bedroom, to the bathroom and helped me shower nearly every day for years.

I had to take more and more medication just to mask some of the pain. Because of this, there were many days where I was not even cognitively aware of what was going on around me. It was terrible. I was unable to do anything, let alone participate in family events like Thanksgiving, Christmas, birthdays, etc. Mark would cook the meals, get the kids ready and then come up to our bedroom, carry me downstairs and set me up at the table. However, I was so heavily medicated that I was not present mentally.

I felt like I was losing everything. I was completely uninvolved. I was in a very bad, dark place. It was so **frustrating and depressing** for me to watch my life pass me by, while I was powerless to join in. Being stuck in bed all the time meant that I could not participate or enjoy my family the way I desperately wanted. I was not able to create memories with my family. Here, I had ten kids that I loved so much, and because of my disabling pain, I was unable to spend quality time with them. It was devastating to our entire family.

A TEMPORARY RELIEF WITH AN UGLY DOWNSIDE

Eventually, we found something that could help. We discovered corticosteroid shots. I started getting those quarterly, but I didn't realize all the risks that are associated with them. Before my first shot, I asked about the risks. However, the doctor administering my shots did not tell me or was not aware of all the side effects.

I've been receiving them for seven years now. They're only supposed to be temporary because, over time, they can actually cause osteoporosis, memory problems, adrenal fatigue, and weight problems. They can also contribute to anxiety and depression. Worse still is the fact that the benefits don't last very long. They would only relieve some of the pain for a couple of weeks, maybe three to four at the most. This treatment is limited as I would not be able to get another shot for twelve weeks.

Imagine the vicious cycle that I was in. I would receive a shot, recover from the procedure, then after recovery, I was able to move around and do basic things, like walking, for a few weeks. Then slowly I would decline back into my wheelchair. Nobody seemed to understand what I was going through. People judged me quite heavily and commented on my up-and-down cycle. Some people even told me that I was faking it just to get attention. Ouch!

A CHRISTMAS GIFT THAT CHANGED OUR LIFE

Our life changed on Christmas Day, 2012. My mother-in-law, Mark's mom, gave us some essential oils. I had heard of essential oils. I wasn't really sure what they were or how they worked. She had given us a **"doTERRA family physicians kit"** as a gift. After receiving these oils, I was intrigued and literally could not put them down. I wanted to learn everything I could about how to use them.

I studied the booklet that came with them every day. As I was looking through the pages, I read that "tea tree" oil could remove warts. Well, I had a wart on my finger I'd had for years that I couldn't get rid of and decided to try it. I'm glad I did because after using just two drops a day, it was gone in two weeks and didn't even leave a scar! I couldn't believe it. I got very excited about these naturally powerful oils because they actually worked. I had to learn more!

THE MIRACLE OF HELICHRYSUM

In the fall of 2013, I had the opportunity to go to an essential oil convention in Salt Lake City. I went down in my wheelchair. On the second day of the convention, I went to a breakout session where the instructor taught the characteristics of the oil, **Helichrysum.** She said it could help with my pain. Skeptically, I tried it that night, and to my surprise, I actually slept. For the first time in months, I slept the whole night. It was fantastic! I used the oil again the next day and incredibly, I did not need my wheelchair. Not knowing how long the effects would last, we brought the wheelchair to have it "just in case." I sat in it for the morning session of the convention, and at lunch, I was able to get up. Now, sitting for that long and then walking afterwards never happened for me. The fact that I was actually able to get up and walk was **my own personal miracle.**

I decided to leave the wheelchair right where it was and told my friends that I wanted to go wander and explore my new-found mobility. I never dreamed I'd be able to walk like this again and now thanks to these oils, I was able to walk wherever I wanted. I spent 8 hours in meetings that day and every time I needed to get up and walk I did! That evening, I went to another meeting and I even climbed stairs, which was just crazy for me. The next day we left for home. It was a fourteen-hour-long car ride. Driving long distances was always very hard on me. Getting up and walking when we stopped for gas and food would always be a challenge. Typically, in order for me to get out of the car, Mark would have to lift me out and into my wheelchair. On this trip home, I was able to get out and walk on my own at every single stop. Even more incredible was that when we got home from that long drive, I was able to help carry in the luggage!

GETTING MY LIFE BACK

These oils have changed our lives. I have expanded my regimen and now layer **Helichrysum, Frankincense, Clove, DDR Prime** and **Deep Blue Rub** on my spine. I also added in the whole food supplement **"Lifelong Vitality,"** which is the foundation of an ultimately healthy lifestyle. Now I've been able to do way more in my life than before. Of course, there are still many things that I cannot do, but by and large, I have my life back!

Here's another miracle. In 2018, my husband surprised me for our anniversary by taking us on an incredible trip to climb Machu Picchu in Peru! It had been on my dream bucket list since high school, and because of my degenerative back pain, I had given up on that dream. I could never see it happening with the way my body was breaking down. Thanks to these precious essential oils, I have aspired once again to open up all my dreams and keep dreaming; and more than just dream about things, I am actually able to accomplish them!

UNDERSTANDING THE DIFFERENT QUALITY STANDARDS OF ESSENTIAL OILS

One thing that I really want to be clear on is the fact that not all essential oils have the same quality, potency, or therapeutic value. There is a direct connection between your results and the quality of the essential oil you use. How they are ethically and sustainably sourced are also important because proper methods of growing, harvesting, and distilling essential oils are crucial.

Basically, there are four different standards of oil quality:

1.) The first standard is primarily for use in the perfume industry. These oils are typically synthetic (which is why many people react to them) or have been altered and have no, or limited, therapeutic value. They are often used in bath and body type of products.
2.) The second standard is "Therapeutic Grade," which means that each chemical compound is within the right therapeutic percentage for that oil. However, this standard does not take into account the purity of the oil.

3.) The third standard is GRAS (Generally Regarded As Safe). This means that the oil can be used as a food additive. These are standardized, which means they are either completely or partially synthetic.

4.) The fourth, and highest standard, was created by doTERRA. "Certified Pure Therapeutic Grade (CPTG) is a whole new standard of quality to support health and wellness. These oils undergo detailed testing by third-party laboratories. They test for fillers, synthetics, and additives. If present, those oils are rejected. They are also tested for their Therapeutic Value. No other oils are more **tested and trusted** for their purity and effectiveness. The Latin name doTERRA means "Gift of the Earth".

TAKEAWAYS FOR A HAPPY, HEALTHY YOU

—Consider looking into the natural, powerful benefits of CPTG essential oils to help with your pain. They are so easy to use every day.

—Good food is your foundation. Certain foods can reduce inflammation and alleviate depression and stress.

—Exercise! Start small and work your way toward small goals. Movement of any kind will serve you far more than if you are sedentary.

—Have a great mindset! What you think is how you feel. Your thoughts and feelings have an unbelievable connection with your pain. What are *you* thinking?

—Manage your stress. It was stress that initially caused the first problems with my back. Do something you love that makes you happy today (dancing, yoga, etc.).

LIVE ON HOPE

Never give up on your dreams. Take a lesson from our personal story of not being able to walk to climbing Machu Picchu, pain-free. Remember, even when it looks like the odds are stacked against you, there is still hope.

I have recaptured my life. You can too. These oils have helped to manage my pain and returned the freedom I had lost. I have been able to get my life back and accomplish things I never thought possible. As we continue to learn and master these oils, our goal is to put them into every home and empower you to have hope, unlock your success, and live your dreams.

We are living proof that these oils can help you in the big five areas of your life: physical, mental/emotional, spiritual, career, and financial.

We are on a journey to **reinvent health care**. We are HopeNaturalWellness.ca, and our mission is to change the world one drop, one person, one community at a time.

About Mark & Kathryn

Kathryn graduated from CanScribe Career College in 2011 with High Honors in Medical Transcription. She returned to school in 2017 at the Health Coach Institute and became a Certified Holistic Health and Lifestyle Coach, graduating in 2018. As a post-graduate student, she is deepening her skills as a "Master of Habit Change." Kathryn loves food and is attending the Canadian School of Natural Nutrition to become a Certified Holistic Nutrition Consultant, to graduate with honors in 2020. She is also a Wellness Advocate and Essential Oil Expert and Educator.

Kathryn was once in a wheelchair due to a crippling back disease. She struggled with depression, weight gain, and disabling pain. In 2012, Mark and Kathryn received essential oils as a gift which changed their lives forever. Through the power of the essential oils, hope opened up possibilities once lost. Her greatest triumph happened in 2018 when she and Mark lived out her dream of climbing Machu Picchu! A dream she had completely given up on. As a best-selling author and speaker, she is looking forward to completing her new book, *"From Wheelchair To Machu Picchu."*

When Kathryn speaks, her passion shines through as she talks about health, nutrition and essential oils. She inspires and empowers others to dream, to reopen possibilities that once felt hopeless. With her experiences and education as a Master of Habit Change, she helps clients cope with and/or reduce stress, and get amazing results.

Mark served a mission in the Eastern United States in 1979, falling in love with its people and their amazing history; he graduated from Southern Alberta Institute of Technology with honors as a Master Gasfitter/Plumber in 1984 and served 35 years in the Boy Scouts of Canada receiving many of their top awards. Mark cultivates a strong sense of community as a founding member of the local C.O.P. chapter (Citizen's On Patrol). He inspires growth and creativity as a long-time director/producer with the local Musical Theatre and served as its President and other various leadership responsibilities for 27 years. Mark is a Block Parent and has coached soccer, basketball and served many years as a referee. Mark enjoys history and served on the Historical Society board for a number of years.

In his free time Mark is a blogger, researcher, international speaker, trainer, bestselling author, mindset builder, Wellness Advocate, world traveler and has a love for nature. Mark is retiring from his 35-year career to move into speaking full-time so as to share his message of hope, and mindset using his marvelous gift of humor. Mark's greatest interest is in the use of essential oils and how their frequencies can lift your mood, clear your mind, raise your spirits, support your health, align your thoughts, and an infinite number of other possibilities. "In order to change your life, you must first change your mind."

Mark and Kathryn were both born, raised and live in rural Southern Alberta where they raised their ten children.

- HopeNaturalWellness@gmail.com
- EssentialKitty.ca
- WannaBuyASundial@gmail.com
- HopeNaturalWellness.ca

CHAPTER 17

THE REAL ESTATE *WHISPERER*

BY JOHN BOBNES

When I was asked to write a chapter for this book, I was honored. Self-improvement is a cornerstone of human development and growth, and being able to contribute is a responsibility I take very seriously. The idea that something I write may resonate with you and help you achieve your heart's desire is the best payment I could hope for.

I was raised by a single mom who worked a lot. I spent countless hours soaking up life lessons from my Depression-era grandparents, Kathryn and Vincent. I spent most of my time with them. They were huge proponents of continuing education and always encouraged me to read anything I could get my hands on. They were tough on me. They didn't waste a penny, and if I wanted something, I was told I had to earn it.

Reading helped build character, fine tune my moral compass and influenced my development into the man I am today. Through reading, I went on fantastic adventures and learned valuable life lessons on the pages of classic novels and often my grandfather's old-school sales training manuals.

My grandmother used to tell me that the best way to learn about something was to do it and to spend time with those that are the best at it. Determined to try to find the one "answer" for how others became "successful," I interviewed 50 highly successful people. The first thing I learned from the extensive interviews was "success" is as unique to everyone as a fingerprint. Secondly, I learned that there wasn't just one answer, but more like nine. I call them the **Life Lessons for Success**. I also learned that there was one consistent overlap from every person with whom I spoke. I'll reveal that later.

I was taught early on by my grandfather, the *best* salesperson I've ever known, that to be a successful salesperson, I needed to listen to my customers and clearly identify their timing and motivation. In my 25-plus-year sales career, I've spent far more time discussing my customer's "heart's desire," than the actual product I was selling them.

Have you ever taken a few minutes to stop and truly define what success looks like for you?

I presume that if you are reading a book about *The Success Formula*, you do not yet consider yourself "Successful." Is that fair? So first, please take a minute and answer the following question:

What would it will look like if you could say you are truly "successful?" Please finish this sentence:
To be successful, I _____ .

LIFE LESSONS FOR SUCCESS

<u>Life Lesson for Success #1</u> – **"The world doesn't owe you anything!"** I remember my grandparents repeatedly telling me to lose my sense of entitlement. At the time, it felt a bit harsh, but their hearts were in the right place.   If you accept the fact that you are going to have to work hard to get what you truly desire, from that day forward no one will ever out-work you!

Life Lesson for Success #2 – "Identify your heart's desire!"
It's the thing you'd run into a burning building to find. One of the best Realtors of all time, my mentor, Craig Proctor said, "A man will struggle to work to pay his bills, but that same man will move mountains for his heart's desire!"

Take a second and ask yourself, "What is your proverbial *WHY?*" When you work for that *WHY*, you won't dread Mondays anymore!

Some say material things make them *successful*, and some don't. While shiny things are lovely, would that really mean those folks are successful? Honestly, if that's how *they* define success, then who's to argue?

For me, success is much more than just a fancy sports car. I'd be more inclined to say being successful means I raised children that make the world a better place.

Seeds of character were planted in me as a young child. I can still hear my grandfather's voice encouraging me to live by the "Golden Rule," and be mindful of my "legacy." Those seeds grew and became the foundation of who I am, today. My life is one dedicated to service and taking care of other people—whether it's my children, friends or clients.

Helping my fellow man uplift and elevate their own lives is the currency of *my* success.

Imagine what the world would be like if all seven billion of us worked to elevate and uplift one another.

Only you can define the currency of *your* success. Whatever it is, you will likely have to do things differently to get different results. It may be uncomfortable, but you can do it.

Life Lesson for Success #3 – **"Do not put it off another day!"**
I'm as guilty of procrastination as anyone.

George Washington said, "99% of failures come from people who have the habit of making excuses."

It's a little cliché, but please, "seize the day!" There is no *perfect time* to do anything, so do it now. Again, change will be uncomfortable, but there is no growth without discomfort. If you don't keep growing, you die. We are all only here for a short time. I encourage you not to waste another precious second. You have the power to make yourself successful. Make at least one decision daily, to make that a reality.

My uncle, also named Vincent, died at the age of 40 in a freak airplane accident, my sister drowned in a swimming pool at the age of two, and my mother passed away suddenly in 2012. She was a young 67, healthy looking and active. She got pneumonia one day and died shortly after. The suddenness and lack of warning shook me. Reflecting on the finality of death, I was suddenly haunted by the two sayings: "You can't take it with you," and, "You aren't promised tomorrow, so make the most of today."

We will all be on our proverbial death bed one day. After my Mom's death, I imagined for a moment I was there, looking back with either regret or contentment. The thought of being there at the end, feeling regret, stung. The thought that I'd want to go back and change things, and knowing that it was too late, was horrifying. I knew that when that day comes (and it will come), I would only want to feel contentment. I asked myself, "Will I be proud to be known as the man that accumulated the most stuff and who had the most money, or would I prefer to have a legacy of helping others and leaving the world a better place?" That simple question has helped guide my daily decisions since then.

I feel like those I cared about most who had passed away, had given me the gift of clarity.

I'm not saying a Lamborghini wouldn't be great, but for me, "success" is a life lived helping others. In fact, being charitable is one of the reasons I started my own real estate company in southern California in 2018. I quadrupled my real estate business from 2016 to 2017 and tripled it again from 2017 to 2018, but the thing I take the most pride in is, with my customers' help, I've personally given more to charity in 2018 than I have the previous 25 years combined. We donate $500 of our commission from every transaction, in our customer's name, to either the Wounded Warrior Project, charity:water or Children's Hospital-Los Angeles. Knowing we are helping save children's lives and helping wounded heroes and bringing clean water to those without it, drives me to be the best in my field.

Life Lesson for Success #4 – "Just focus on today, and the rest of your life will take care of itself." ~ Kathryn Bobnes

Take it one day at a time. Do one small thing daily, to get to where you want to be. Over time, all of those small things will have paved your road to success.

Life Lesson for Success #5 – "Have a goal (direction) and steadily work toward it!" Write down your goal. Your goal should state where you want to see yourself in the next five years, ten years, and beyond. That's where it all begins, and if you continue to push forward toward it steadily, your life will change forever, for the better. Henry David Thoreau said, "Go confidently in the direction of your dreams. Live the life you have imagined." That's the answer to *HOW* you become what success means to you. You must first imagine and then act.

Things were not always good for me. As a matter of fact, in my late 30's, I was struggling in a failing marriage with a violent spouse with life-long dependency issues. I was obese, I didn't feel satisfied or appreciated at work, and felt like my life was slipping away without purpose. I had hit my limit. I heard my grandfather in my head telling me, "You're not a passenger on a train. You have a say in the direction your life goes." I decided no matter how hard or uncomfortable, I wasn't going to live that way, or that life, anymore!

I decided to follow my heart's desire.

Life Lesson for Success #6 – "Take risks!" (...preferably take calculated ones!)

> *The ONLY strategy that is GUARANTEED TO FAIL*
> *is not taking risks!*
> ~ Mark Zuckerberg

Earlier in the chapter, I referenced an "overlap" common to all 50 successful people I interviewed. After each of them identified what exactly they wanted for their lives and what would make them feel genuinely *successful*, the consensus was that they ALL had to change their routine to get the results they were looking for and, most importantly, they had to forge ahead continually.

To change my path, I decided to change my routine drastically. I went into therapy to regain my focus and to take ownership of the situation I was in. I started eating right and exercising, plus, I committed to reading a self-improvement book every week. I lost 60 pounds in about six months, and I worked a full-time job to pay the bills while I studied every night for a year to get my real estate license. I fought and won full custody of my kids. I got my real estate license, trained with one of the most successful Realtors in the world, and began to work toward my goal of being part of a real estate company that's sole focus was to help others. The problem was, the real estate company I was working for at the time, and every other real estate company I looked at working with, didn't have that same focus. I took a huge risk, found a great location, and The Bobnes Group Real Estate was born!

I dedicated my company to my grandparents who taught me the value of hard work and "always putting the customer first." I now own a successful company employing great, like-minded people that always help others in the process.

What if you take risks and fail, you ask? Don't worry, you will fail. That's ok. As a matter of fact, that might be better.

The past teaches the lessons to implement in the future!

Learn from your mistakes and come back stronger!

Life Lesson for Success #7 – "Stop worrying!" There's an old Japanese proverb that says: "If a problem CAN be solved, then it's not worth worrying about. If a problem CAN'T be solved, then it too, is useless to worry about!"

You have wasted too much time worrying! I wish I would have internalized the "worry is worthless" message decades ago. I would have saved myself tremendous anguish. Please absorb and adopt that message. Good *will* happen. Bad *will* happen. When you deal with the realities of life, worry is the lead jacket that makes it harder to maneuver around the obstacles along the way.

Life Lesson for Success #8 – "Be the (whatever is your passion) Whisperer!" My grandfather told me when I was young that whatever I chose to do, to be the best at it. Self-improvement helps you on your path to be the best version of yourself, but more importantly, it helps those around you be better too. For me, the better I am, the more clients and worthy causes I can help. I encourage you to "Be the (whatever is your passion) *Whisperer*" as much for others, as for yourself!

Life Lesson for Success #9 – "Be generous!"
Successful people are always looking for opportunities to help others.
Unsuccessful people are always asking, "What's in it for me?"
~ Brian Tracy

A wise man once told me, "The size of the hole you give out

of is directly proportionate to the size of the hole you receive through!" I donate more money and time to charity now than I ever have in my life, and I have never made more money, had more time, or more blessings than I do now.

Here are the nine steps on the road to _your_ success:

1. **"The world doesn't owe you anything!"**
2. **"Identify your heart's desire!"**
3. **"Do not put it off another day!"**
4. **"Just focus on today, and the rest of your life will take care of itself."**
5. **"Have a goal (direction) and steadily work toward it!"**
6. **"Take risks!"**
7. **"Stop worrying!"**
8. **"Be the (whatever is your passion) _Whisperer!_"**
9. **"Be generous!"**

In 2017, I was paid the most valuable compliment I've ever received when my 92-year-old grandmother told me that, "I couldn't have imagined, when I held you as a baby, you could become such a great, successful man. Your grandfather would be so proud, and I am blessed to have a grandson like you." She peacefully passed away a few months later in my arms. Those words mean more to me than all the awards and recognition I've received over the years.

She was right, I am successful, and you can be too.

About John

John Bobnes helps his clients create wealth, selling their properties for the most possible, the fastest, with the least hassle possible, and helping them buy real estate smarter.

Heavily influenced by his grandparents, John has a strong moral compass, tremendous work ethic and an appreciation of what is most important in life. With his grandfather's mentoring, John was surrounded by real estate and sales throughout his childhood. Loving science fiction, computers, and electronics as a child, it makes sense that John's business is state-of-the-art and uses cutting-edge real estate technology. Their stunning and creative marketing pieces shine, showcasing John's artistic and creative side while being complemented by complex marketing campaigns and tactical pricing—likely stemming from John's love of playing strategic games of chess.

John learned quickly that he had an affinity for sales and studied hard to rise to the top of his industry. He's been a professional sales manager and trainer for over 20 years. Reading helped him develop his skills and learn from examples set by the likes of John H. Patterson, Dale Carnegie, Zig Ziglar, and modern-day real estate gurus like Craig Proctor.

As a teenager, John's grandfather would regularly tell him, "Whatever you choose to do, be the best at it. Be an expert in your field. Buy a home as soon as possible." and, "Always put your customer first!" Those sentences sparked a passion in John for real estate. He was driven to be the best in California and founded a company that provides unmatched services, guarantees in writing and filled with happy, like-minded agents all putting customers' needs first.

In 2014, John identified many things missing in the real estate field that were crippling efficiency, hurting productivity, and negatively impacting the customers' experience. He started training realtors to improve the sales process and was able to suggest cutting edge technologies to improve service.

Encouraged by other real estate professionals, in 2015, John decided to get his real estate license. In February 2016, John became a licensed realtor and began working with an established brokerage. Unfortunately, like most California agencies, they had very few benefits for their buyer or seller clients beyond having the ability to fill out a contract – offering little in the way of agent development and training.

Knowing there had to be a better way, John sought out some of the best minds in real estate and learned from them. He continues to mastermind with these elite individuals today. Their generous guidance combined with his tremendous sales pedigree helped encourage him down a path to open his own company in 2018, and becoming known among his peers as "The Real Estate Whisperer." Being charitable is exceptionally important to John and is a cornerstone of his business.

His clientele spans the entire spectrum ranging from doctors, lawyers, teachers, entertainment executives and small business owners to Fortune 500 CEOs.

John, a national real estate sales trainer, has shared the stage with some of the top speakers in the real estate world.

You can connect with John at:

- (818) 861-9326 office (call 24/7)
- TheBobnesGroup@gmail.com
- www.facebook.com/TheBobnesGroupRealEstate

CHAPTER 18

ACTIVE WELLNESS IN THE GAME OF LIFE

BY DR. BRAD FREITAG

Are your kids athletes? Are you an athlete, or maybe just a weekend warrior? Do you find achieving wellness difficult at today's pace of life? It's so easy to get caught up in the rat-race and lose track of maintaining one's health! Forget about meditation and relaxation; who has time for that? And what about taking care of everybody else in the family? Between work, housework, grocery shopping, school, sports, and other extra-curriculars, it seems nearly impossible to keep everyone well. And what if the unthinkable does happen . . . an injury significant enough to sideline you or your athlete? Sometimes even when people try to do everything right, they still get injured and are sidelined for weeks, if not months.

When an athlete is removed from his/her sport due to injury, it is important to recognize the significant mental impact this may also have. The same is true for all of us with respect to sustaining injuries and experiencing chronic pain. It takes us "out of the game" and can set us up for lifelong depression and disability. So how do you keep your student-athlete and the rest of your family well amidst today's non-stop, chaotic pace of life?

I believe there are six key components to keeping your athlete [and your entire family] healthy and well:

1. Chiropractic Care: In my opinion, you will get a valuable "bang for your buck" in maintaining your family's wellness by receiving regular chiropractic care. This is largely why most collegiate and professional sports teams have at least one chiropractor on staff. Doctors of Chiropractic remove nerve interference due to misaligned bones/joints in your body - either in your spine, extremities (shoulder, elbow, hip, knee, ankle) or both.

By correcting the misalignments and restoring proper nerve function, a chiropractor is able to improve the range of motion of the affected joint, relax tight musculature, improve strength and coordination, and decrease pain and inflammation. What human doesn't want to be faster, stronger, more flexible, and have less pain? Because your central nervous system (brain, spinal cord, and nerves) controls every cell in your body, a chiropractor can influence every system throughout the body, thereby helping to improve breathing, sleeping, digestion, immunity, movement, and cognitive clarity. In the event of injury, chiropractic care can also be very effective for pain management, reducing the need for harmful drugs, as well as speeding up the process of healing and facilitating appropriate rehab.

In our clinic, we use the Activator technique to perform gentle, specific chiropractic adjustments. We also offer physiotherapies such as electrical muscle stimulation, ultrasound, laser, myofascial release techniques, Kinesio-taping and more to help every member of the family recover quickly and thoroughly from their injuries. This is extremely important in a society that is living longer. It is getting even more important to protect our mobility so that we do not outlive it and can retain a high quality of life in our later years! How many people do you know limping around in pain or with a joint replacement from "an old sports injury"? In a time where it is not uncommon for people to live into their 90's or more, this makes maintaining spinal alignment and mobility exponentially more important [beginning from a young age] to avoid wear and tear. A great maintenance plan for preventative care is to get adjusted one or two times a month.

2. Nutrition: No particular nutritional program is right for everyone, but there are some generalizations that can be applied for most. The simplest way to eat healthy [in theory, not including the willpower needed to actually do it], is to eat "real food," first and foremost. This means avoiding processed foods full of additives and preservatives. A general rule of thumb: get your food from the outside aisles of the grocery store and avoid the middle. This approach should leave your cart filled with lean protein, veggies, fruits, nuts, and seeds, and it will naturally help keep your body alkaline and uninflamed, reducing disease and pain. Likewise, the more you keep your food sources organic and local, the better.

After researching nutrition and wellness for 20 years, I am comfortable with including meat in our diets, as long as it is lean and chemical free, with most of the meat coming in the form of wild-caught fish or game, cage-free chicken, and limited consumption of red meat (once or twice a week). Vegetables should be the largest portion of every meal, with an emphasis on dark-green, leafy vegetables. Some I enjoy and recommend are kale, spinach, broccoli, brussels sprouts, cauliflower, beets, and carrots. Fruit consumption is best kept to berries, as they are lowest in natural sugar, but certainly, limited quantities of apples, oranges, pineapples, and cherries are beneficial as well.

Contrary to common misunderstandings on the topic, a moderate intake of healthy fat is also *key* to good health and wellness. It can also be a valuable source of calories for the active athlete. My go-to's for this are raw nuts (like cashews, pecans, walnuts, hazelnuts, and almonds), avocados, coconut and olive oil, and seeds (such as flax, chia, hemp, and pumpkin). Including a multitude of spices and herbs (garlic, ginger, cinnamon, turmeric, cayenne pepper, basil, rosemary, and so forth) in your cooking is also very tasty and healthy. I also recommend trying to consume all of your meals within a 10-12 hour window each day, ending no later than 8 p.m. This allows your body enough time to perform functions like cellular autophagy - your body's way of cleaning house each day. Research is showing this schedule of eating (called "intermittent fasting") to have profound effects on several important health markers: blood pressure, blood sugar, triglycerides, and cholesterol, as well as positively impacting your body's ability to burn fat as a fuel source, reach deeper/more consistent levels of sleep, and produce more natural growth hormone.

Finally, there are some key supplements that are beneficial to help with obtaining and maintaining a high level of wellness. This topic could easily be its own book, but I will list my top ten recommendations to my patients: a quality multi-vitamin/multi-mineral, Omega-3 oil, probiotic with digestive enzymes, glucosamine, turmeric, vitamin D, magnesium, a greens supplement such as GreensFirst Pro, and amino acids.

3. Hydration: This isn't a very sexy topic, but it is often overlooked. The simple rule-of-thumb: drink half of your body weight in ounces of water every day! Coffee and soda do NOT count. In fact, they can actually negate some of your water intake. Ideally, there would be no consumption of soda, as it contains nothing good for you, but enough sugar and chemicals to make it quite harmful. The debate over coffee and caffeine continues, but most recent research shows an overwhelming agreement that coffee, in moderation of 1-3

cups per day and by itself (no creamers, sweeteners, sugar, or other flavors) can actually be good for you. Disagreement continues with respect to caffeine yet. Upon navigating the research and trying to make an informed decision, five days a week I consume organic, naturally-decaffeinated coffee (1-2 cups/day) and two days per week I consume one cup of organic caffeinated coffee about an hour before my weight-lifting workouts for a little extra boost.

Additional beverages that are healthy to consume are herbal teas and hot water mixed with 1 ounce each of freshly squeezed lemon juice and apple-cider vinegar. On days of significant physical exertion, it may also be necessary to add electrolytes to some of your water. Our bodies are 70-80% water, so it only makes sense that we would work hard every day to replenish it.

4. Exercise: Whether you're a young athlete, older athlete, or weekend warrior, there is some common ground when it comes to approaching exercise. A large part of that common ground is being sure to develop balanced strength and avoid over-training any one muscle group. Regardless of an individual's sport or activity, it is critical to train one's upper body *and* lower body. Strength training can be done with free weights, body weight, kettlebells, resistance bands, or multiple other ways.

In addition to building balanced strength, you must also work to develop and maintain flexibility and proper ranges of motion. Any one of many forms of yoga are great for this, but just a simple stretching routine at home works well, too. This is crucial in the pursuit of injury prevention while active in sports and longevity in the game of life. Some type of cardio appropriate for your level of heart health and fitness is also necessary. However, this does not imply that you must become a runner and register for your first marathon! In fact, some of today's most popular fitness gurus are suggesting much less cardio than previously thought to enjoy the myriad of benefits. Just a few examples of cardio are walking, running, biking, hiking, HIIT (high-intensity interval training), Zumba, sprint training, snowshoeing, or cross-country skiing.

Additional common ground in everyone's exercise regimen should be balance training. This is another one crucial to injury prevention and longevity. One of the simplest ways to work on balance is to practice balancing on one foot while standing on different surfaces of stability. You can then repeat the exercise, but with your eyes closed, to further increase the difficulty and engage more of your body's neuromuscular proprioception.

The final piece of common ground with physical activity is REST. One of the most prevalent causes of injury I see in my clinic is from overuse or overtraining. Today's young athletes are either playing multiple sports all year or specializing in one sport all year in school and then in traveling leagues for that sport the rest of the year. As weekend warriors or parents of athletes, this equates to being short on time. As a result, we often cram too much physical activity into short periods of time. To avoid injury and foster our best life possible [at any age], we must make time to rest between activity.

5. Sleep: Staying on the topic of rest, every human needs quality sleep each night to be their best, ranging from 7-8 hours for adults and 8-10 hours for teenagers. Although this isn't always possible, there are a few suggestions to help improve your quality of sleep. Most of these tips are things that will help reinforce your natural circadian rhythm [your 24-hour wake/sleep cycle]. In this digital age, it is very important to keep technology out of your bedroom. Many devices emit sounds and light that can disturb you from getting deep sleep.

There is also research that shows our devices emit low-level radiation that can disrupt our melatonin levels, a hormone we need to sleep. If possible, be sure to use blackout curtains over your bedroom windows to block out all light. Avoid sugar and caffeine after 2 p.m. Maintain a cool temperature, as this will signal your body to sleep and sleep deeper. To amplify this effect, take a quick, hot shower or use a hot tub or sauna just before bed. Then, as your body cools off while preparing for bed, that will also signal to the body/brain that it's time for sleep.

Avoid screen time for 1-2 hours before going to bed, as the blue light emitted via the screen signals to your brain that it is daytime and you should feel awake and energized. It is also very helpful to your body to have a common bedtime and wake time each day, and a routine is also beneficial in training your body for deep and productive sleep. My preferred bedtime routine to prepare for sleep is a soak in the hot tub, and then for about 30 minutes while my body cools off, I sip herbal tea and read in soft light.

6. Mental Management: Personally, this is the key component that I struggle most to find time for in my day. This includes things like journaling, praying, meditating, visualizing, performing affirmations, goal-setting, self-reflecting, and any other activity designed to keep our minds focused on the "bigger picture" that helps us become the best version of ourselves. It comprises a host of activities that we need to do to de-stress, stay positive, be focused on who we are, and know what we are passionate about.

This component requires us to *sslllooooowwww* down, which in today's world is critical, but so difficult to do. It requires us to be intentional. There are thousands of wonderful resources online, three of my favorites being: mindvalley.com, mylifebook.com, and darrenhardy.com.

When incorporating these six components of wellness into the game of life, everybody's game plan is going to look different, but the goal would be to follow this basic template. For those of you working 2nd or 3rd shift, you'll just need to "shift" the times of day. Your day should start with some water, 5-10 minutes of journaling or meditation, and exercise. Short on time, do a 15 minute HIIT video at home. You should consume water throughout your day (in between meals, but not after dinner) in an amount equal to half of your body weight in ounces. Around 7 or 8 a.m., have a healthy breakfast and take supplements. Between 11 a.m. – 1 p.m., have a healthy lunch with supplements, then spend 5-10 minutes doing creative visualizations and/or affirmations. If time allows, take a quick walk outside or do some simple yoga poses or stretching, 10-15 minutes is better than nothing. Some days it will work in the schedule, some days it won't. Don't sweat the small stuff!

The after school/work time usually gets broken down into the 3 - 6 shift and 6 - 9 shift. What happens during those times depends mostly on your family's schedule of events and commitments. Schedule-pending, this time may include a workout or mental-management. You'll also prep a healthy dinner during these hours, and it is essential to finish eating by 7 or 8 p.m. so that everyone can have at least 12 hours of intermittent fasting between dinner and breakfast. Don't forget supplements with dinner.

Once or twice a month, don't forget to incorporate a chiropractic visit to maintain your overall wellness. By now, it's time for a quick hot shower, sauna session, or hot-tub soak followed by relaxing with herbal tea while reading or listening to music to prepare for bed. Try to avoid screen time after 7 p.m. If that's not possible, at least wear blue-blockers. These are similar to sunglasses and block the damaging blue light from reaching your eyes and signaling to your brain that it is still day time and you should be awake, not sleepy. In your dark and cool room, get into bed by 10 p.m. with no technology, and wake by 6 a.m. the next day to do it all over again. Repeat and live your absolute, best life possible!

Decide today to make time for health, so later you don't have to make time for illness. In the words of Herophilus, "When health is absent, wisdom cannot reveal itself, art cannot manifest, strength cannot fight, wealth becomes useless, and intelligence cannot be applied."

About Dr. Brad

Dr. Brad Freitag is a second-generation chiropractor who has been helping athletes of all ages and their families obtain their healthiest lives possible for 18 years. Dr. Brad owns and operates his own wellness clinic, employing multiple doctors and staff who serve a mission to help as many people as possible live their best life using natural, alternative healthcare such as chiropractic and nutritional therapy. Especially in a time where many people are outliving their mobility and not ending with a desirable quality of life, he strives to educate young athletes and their families on the importance of injury prevention and whole-body wellness that he not only preaches but also practices.

Dr. Freitag received his Bachelor of Science degree from the UW-Madison and his Doctorate of Chiropractic from Palmer College of Chiropractic in Davenport, Iowa. He graduated *magna cum laude*, was given the distinction of being on the President's List, and was awarded membership to Pi Tau Delta, the International Chiropractic Honor Society.

Dr. Brad is an avid reader and outdoor-enthusiast, residing in his hometown of Monticello near Madison, with his wife and two children.

You can connect with Dr. Brad at:

- info@bellevillechiropractic.net
- www.bellevillechiro.com
- www.facebook.com/bellevillechiropractic&wellness

CHAPTER 19

THE SUCCESS REFLEX

BY JOHN BRAVE

There I lay, flat on my back with the wind knocked clean out of my lungs, looking up at the ceiling, waiting for my hearing to fully return. My Sifu (Kung-Fu teacher), reaches out and helps me to my feet. He motions to me to try the move again, except during this set he parries left, instead of right. We go for several more rounds, but each time he responds differently. He pivots, he deflects, he side steps, and feigns. No matter what I do, I can't seem to get through his defenses, or his offenses for that matter! In my utter frustration, after endless failed attempts, I finally ask him, "Sifu, how am I supposed to master this move if you behave differently every single time?" His response puzzled me back then, but little did I know, that it would later become the basis for my business leadership training methodology. In fact, it would become my overall approach to success in life on a whole! The years I spent training saved me in so many ways. Though you wouldn't know it if you looked at me today, I spent half my life believing that I was the black sheep of my family. My siblings were all extremely academically gifted. They attended country day schools, boarding schools and Ivy League universities. I, however, was the polar opposite.

Being stamped as a perpetually distracted, problem kid with clinically-diagnosed learning issues (ADHD), who needed chemical assistance just to sit still, yet I was determined to learn to chase down success by alternative means. I translated what I learned in the martial arts as a means of teaching myself new things. It helped me to focus my mind more sharply and to start to instill self-discipline. Surprisingly, it also helped me to develop the ability to think multidimensionally. Now, to some people, that might just sound like a fancy quantum mechanics word, but to put it plainly, through practicing the mental and physical discipline of Kung-Fu, I learned to draw from my past, stay in the moment, yet anticipate the future simultaneously.

To a young boy who was always challenged in school, developing the ability to face an opponent (or a situation), by entering a mental state where time seemed to be moving in slow motion, to pro-act instead of react, made me feel superhuman. This was also known as the "Flow State" in neuropsychology and consciousness studies, "The Zone" in the high- performance athletics and "Heightened Awareness" in the military.

Soon after, I became obsessed with something that was an unexpected but perfect complement to the ancient eastern practices I was learning...quantum physics. Studying concepts like synchronicity, observer subjective reality and superposition allowed me to hack my own brain long before it was even a common term. Suffice it to say, I was an outcast. Growing up struggling to understand myself, I realized that I was being viewed in a way that was not congruent with how I saw myself. I always wanted to do something important yet I always felt marginalized. After escaping the perceived torture of academia, I thrust myself into work life. I started out with the most menial jobs that I had to work extremely hard to obtain. I had a deep appreciation for everything I earned, so I felt lucky to be cleaning and scraping whatever I was asked to. This attitude would prove to serve me well.

Fast forward one decade and one divorce later – years after I had embarked upon a career in retail – I found myself skyrocketing from one level of management to another. Whenever I was faced with do-or-die situations, instead of crumbling under the pressure, I almost always rose to the occasion, to my own surprise. I was further surprised when sharing my ideas and thoughts during interdepartmental meetings, that people found them to be unorthodox and radical yet they were met with rousing enthusiasm. My training methods were seen as unusual, yet my supervisors were highly curious as to how I obtained such consistently-enhanced results.

As head of training and development for my division, I had the good fortune of working alongside some of the brightest minds in the industry. Part of my secret sauce was that I frequently made a point to pick the big brains of other department heads. Many of the techniques we vetted were based on neuropsychology and cognitive learning models, which allowed people to learn faster, retain more deeply and execute closer to standard from the start. In facilitating these sessions, I began to develop a reputation as a consummate trainer and natural HR talent. I soon possessed a pride that later became my deadly sin. I became a taskmaster and strategy execution junkie. There I was, striving at a peak in my career, thinking that I was hitting this management thing out of the park and that my Mother and my Sifu would be proud.

My rude awakening came in the form of a leadership feedback survey that I implemented. I discovered that my team's perception of me was the exact opposite of what I believed. I was ignorant of my arrogance, thinking I was a man of the people within my company. I thought I was an enlightened conscious corporateer, only to find out that I was actually perceived as a tyrannical boss. That's right...a boss-hole!

I was dumbfounded when I discovered that my nickname was "The Terminator" because my people felt I had an itchy trigger finger. Apparently, I was quick to put people on written corrective action at the very first misstep, all the way up to termination, in record time. I had no idea that my management style was so toxically stringent. I had amazing relationships with my management peer group and my own supervisors, meanwhile the people who were supposed to trust me to lead them, were mostly suffering under my rigidity. I thought that my disciplined approach to business was the way to do business because, well... business is business. There was no room for individual emotion! I was collective-minded but still not quite people-minded. I was so mission-driven that I forgot who the mission was for.

I needed to learn to separate from my ego, advocate for my people and repair the damage. I always envisioned myself as an amazing manager...as I said, I was in complete ignorance of my own arrogance. I learned the hard way that my people never needed a manager but were searching for a leader. Over the next few years, needless to say, or perhaps much needed to be said, I fully recalibrated and immersed myself in every manner of transformational leadership training I could get into – from Tony Robins to Zig Ziglar and even the Dalai Lama.

So when people talk about transformation, for me, it's not just a platitude. I learned so much very early on about myself and achievement, but was missing a very big piece of the puzzle due to diving too deeply into the sea of my own ego. According to Robert Townsend, the author of the acclaimed book, *Up The Organization*, if you push a bundled up chain there is no way to predict which way it will go. But if you take one end and simply pull it, then it will follow you wherever you lead it. Many have said before that great leaders take point and lead from the front. Courage was the signature of true leadership.

In learning this, I made a point only to work for companies that had actively involved founders, so that I could master the principles of invoking culture clarity and heightened levels of workplace morale—leading to record levels of employee engagement. Of course, the aforementioned renders an entire assortment of additional calculable and incalculable benefits, like decreased attrition, fewer call outs, lowered stress with an increased sense of challenge and fulfillment, attracting higher quality candidates, the company being perceived as an employer of choice, deeper levels of loyalty, productivity, of course revenue and dare I say even a bit of playful fun from time to time. All of this had become who I was as a leader. Instead of me priding myself, my team was proud of me for being a leader who would not let a strategy go forward unless there was the right energy, emotion and human spirit to power it!

I stopped using will power and started using "Why" power! Without first examining our motives, (the powerful reason why), and if it really serves the many vs. the few, nothing can truly move forward in good conscience. Today, I train leaders and their teams to feel uncomfortable within the comfort zone, effectively reducing, eliminating and strategically reverse polarizing what is known as the inner receptivity field. Thereby, sensitizing a person to feel stagnant when they're not growing and leveling up through exciting and worthwhile challenges; making success practically a reflex action. Your positive habits transcend into a much more rapid response and highly agile mental strength tool that you control vs. having random emotional reactions control you.

This is the nature of how to develop what I call, The Success Reflex™. A state of mind, a state of ability and a state of being that brings out the very best in a person, both in their life and in their work. Furthermore, it endeavors to empower every person to "entrepreneurialize" their jobs and take on a level of leadership responsibility within their own sphere to elevate themselves and their team with passion and with purpose. Here you will find a brief blueprint of the eight transcending formulas within this evolutionary methodology.

1. Decision! The power of the initial decision to forever change things for the better and take honest stock of the present circumstance and continually apply some tough self-love. To confront the harsh reality that things CAN and SHOULD be better - starting from the moment we make a firm decision

to follow through. We call the one decision with so much gravity Your Singularity, for it is the thrust from which all of your subsequent actions are born.

2. Vision! One must cast an epic and collaborative vision. The only mistake here is thinking too small. This must be considered your sacred quest.

3. Mission! Nothing great happens without tapping into failure and then transforming it into the power of triumph. Forge unstoppable goals from a place of immovable conviction.

4. Passion! Igniting passion requires fire in the belly, burning desire! Leverage the power of emotion as the unlimited fuel source that it truly is and master EQ in the process.

5. Action! True visionaries lead the charge but are also ready to step back, let their team take point on certain legs of the mission in order to propel growth and create self-regulation. An atmosphere of accountability, where everyone is the boss of their respective area, allowing leaders to trade supervision for future-vision.

6. Mindset! Sharpening the mind. According to the principle of control, whoever is the most flexible will control the system – not the most rigid. Learn to have a highly adaptive mindset that can assume the most advantageous mental position and triumph in virtually any life situation. Experience and create exponential vertical growth through the quantum thought process.

7. Skillset! We all must rise beyond the occasion and hold ourselves accountable first and foremost to our own highest standard. This is everyone's solemn promise to uphold, that they will bring their very best and ask for and offer support. The entire team actively participates in core skills (horizontal growth) enhancement programs that are activated to empower each person exponentially (vertical growth).

8. Contribution! We all need a sense of purpose, significance and to be celebrated. With empowered development and doing away with performance management of old, we can focus on a synergistic co-created culture.

The prime directive of this final step is repairing and strengthening the connective tissue between workforce and management. To deepen the trust and transparency and powerfully galvanize all levels of the organization as well as each individual team member's career trajectories.

These eight tenets are the Rosetta Stone tablets for unlocking courageous, heart-centered leadership and living a purpose-driven life! Imagine leading a team and living a life where winning was not a long, painful and arduously sacrificial process. Imagine a life where winning is reflexive! How do you get your people to not only put their backs but their hearts into it as well? I mean, we know our people matter, but how do we get them to know how much they really matter to us and to the organizations' success? I've asked and answered all of these questions for myself. And in doing so, I'm proud to say I've built a passionate legacy for unlocking raw human potential and transforming it into refined human possibility. I've spent my lifetime developing these battle-hardened methods for Fortune 500 fashion retail companies. But the revelation is not all mine to claim. It struck me years ago, like lightning, back when I was struggling with ADHD and learning those advanced Kung-Fu techniques.

Flashing back to that day of utter frustration ... my Sifu kept landing me flat on my back, knocking the wind clean out of my lungs ... I finally realized that the reason my Sifu made a point to change his approach continually, was because mastering the ability to react in the moment to all variations of an attack was, in fact, the ONLY way to master the technique in a fashion that it could actually be considered a useable skill. Rote sequences of habitual movements would only fail you in times of real crises for lack of flexibility. This was quantum thinking. You have to train your physiology, prepare your mind and push the threshold of your reflexes. In doing so, your skills grow exponentially. This is the binding principle of all that I learned and later taught to Managers who pledged to become Leaders instead.

Management and Leadership are crucial distinctions with uniquely different purposes, much like Habits and Reflexes. I'll end off with this tongue-in-cheek wisdom of my Sifu's response to me on that fateful day of training, "Habits are essential, they get you onto the court, but it's your reflexes that actually win the game!"

About John

John Brave has a long and storied career spanning 20+ years in HR-focused roles, leading and developing teams within the retail fashion sector for Fortune 500 luxury conglomerates and world-renowned designers such as: Donna Karan, Armani, Kenneth Cole, Tommy Hilfiger, etc. He is passionate about creating powerful work experiences that excite entrepreneurial behaviors in all members of the organization at every level.

His agency's mission is to inspire creative and courageous leadership that empowers their teams by co-creating a culture of synergistic innovation, leading to seismic growth. After working with and training some of the best and brightest, John has honed a unique methodology known as *The Success Reflex™* that merges Ancient Eastern Practices, cutting edge Neuropsychology, and the groundbreaking science of Quantum Mechanics, revealing the truth about the nonexistent barriers of human potential. John's favorite question for new clients, (as Morpheus to their Neo): "The blue pill or the red?"

Learn to sharpen your Success Reflexes. Master the eight (8) principles of life-changing leadership by rebooting, rewiring and reprogramming the greatest biotechnology known to man... the human mind!

CONTACT INFORMATION - To find out more about The Success Reflex Academy or the John Brave Agency:

- Call: 323-285-2075
- Email: livebrave@johnbrave.com
- Website: JohnBrave.com
- IG: Johnbravesuccessreflex
- FB: John Brave
- Podcast: The Success Reflex

CHAPTER 20

FORMULA OF SUCCESS

BY DR. MICHAEL AYZIN

Everyone has a story. This is mine.
~ Dr. Michael Ayzin

What makes one successful?
- One builds a house. Check.
- One plants a tree. Check.
- One raises a son, one great son, at that. Check.

Coming from a very modest, by American standards, middle-class divorced family, what could I, an émigré from the Soviet Union in 1980, expect? What did I have going for me besides the background of being from a professional family? My dad was a dental technician. His life was defined by a 1957 event, when he was a young man, of being interrogated by the KGB for meeting an American girl at the Youth Festival in Moscow. Relationships with foreigners were "discouraged" at that time. I loved him dearly, but always thought of him and made parallels with A. Chekhov's "Man in the Case." My mom, who was a dentist, was supporting our family financially. She was a go getter. It was the only way to make a living then.

Being a curious kid, well beyond my peers' age, I spend a lot of time at my parents' work places. I liked the interactions and experiences I observed there, which influenced my decisions. From the early age I knew what I wanted to do in life. Dentistry was my call.

Time was always very important to me. I met many good people along the way, like Mr. Hughes, Head of the Chemistry department, and Mr. Crawford, Head of the English Department at Hollywood High. I am so grateful to them for seeing some potential in me, and letting me graduate from school in a year and a half. The reason time was very important to me was because I wanted to become somebody. Tony Robbins, well-known self-improvement personality, often refers to his own life when he would take a girl out and pray that she did not order a very expensive item on the menu. Funny (not really), at the same age as he was, I distinctly remember restaurants not being in my vocabulary. Sticking to appetizers with dates became a reality only in late college years, where I was accepted on a scholarship.

When it was time for college, I chose biology as my major. It could be said I did it on purpose. There was not much one could do with that major to make a living in my eyes. I was putting my eggs in one basket, betting, or better to say, narrowing my options to focus on one goal: to be accepted to a dental school. College was just a stepping stone in the plan, devised in my head. The challenge was that we had no means no pay for the education I wanted. Good grades along with USC, private and government scholarships helped along the way.

They say luck is a part of success. I was lucky enough to work along with Dr. Carole Snow while at USC, who contributed to my life immensely and to whom I am hugely grateful for seeing in me then who I am today. Being on the USC Dental School Admission Committee, she gave me a chance, so to speak, to "catch up", and after only two years and NO formal interview I was admitted to the dental school. It was a rarity then, and still is now. What also helped to get me accepted into a dental program was my essay, which I worked on for over 6 months –

From childhood I knew what I wanted to do with my life. I had a great, driving desire to be adentist – confident in myself, dedicated to others, a financially secure person with a big heart and magician's hands – has been a part of me since I was 13 years old. This feeling grew slowly, but progressively during the seven years when I had great exposure to dentistry, by visiting my parents in a dental office, where they worked as a dentist and a dental technician. Everything started when I saw a dentist at work for the first time.

I remember this event as though it happened yesterday. It was not so much an event in a literary sense: nothing really took place, there was no action in which I was involved myself. I was only looking at what was going on as a spectator. That day, I came to the dental office to get an apartment key from my mom. She was not in the office at the moment, and I seated myself at the dentist's chair. Every child at that age wants to be like his parents, wants to imitate them. I was no exception.

As I have already said, my mother was out of the office, so being a curious boy, I turned my eyes to the right, where a man in a white uniform worked with a patient. I did not see the dentist's face (he stood with his back towards me), I could see only his hands. The hands were ordinary hands. One could see the big and muscular, but at the same time, gentle man's hand with long, sharp fingers. Those fingers. They were so virtuous! Turning and twisting, not stopping for a second, they created a fairy tale.

Fascinated by their manipulation I couldn't take my eyes away. I gazed on them. I followed their every movement, like a simple spectator watches a magician performing a trick. The name of the 'magician' was dentist, the name of the trick: treatment of a bad tooth. Like a spectator who wants to catch any hidden movement of the performer to learn the techniques of the trick, I wanted to catch them, just to satisfy my childish interest.

At the time, the doctor was concentrating on his work. With confident movements, he took a small mirror and a pointer, examined the patient's mouth carefully, looked at the negative of the bad tooth, understood the problem and began to "solve" it. Seconds later, a handpiece was in his right hand, and he was making a correct form for the filling. The next moment, the "magician" filled it up with a filling material. Of course, the work took at least a quarter of an hour, but for a child who was fascinated with the work, time didn't have any meaning. I was outside of earthly dimensions just like the viewer, whose eyes were riveted on the object of the magician's work during a long-lasting show.

The job was finished. The performance was over, the curtain was lowered. The naïve spectator left the auditorium stunned by the trick itself and by the fact that he neither understood nor learned the techniques of the trick. On the way home, I wanted to see it again and again. What was more important, I wanted to try to repeat it to get a "feeling" of dentistry, doing it with my own hands – a great desire motivated me.

Later, on many occasions during my volunteer work, I found out that I have sensitivity to the needs of other people and the ability to communicate with the patients. Also, I have good hands, inherited from my father, and excellent perceptual as well as dexterous abilities and craft skills, which cannot be substituted by anything else in the dental profession.

Three months after graduating from USC Dental School, an opportunity to run a dental practice as the only dentist at the facility, fell into my lap. It was an opportunity to learn to rely on myself in challenging situations. I drove one hour (each way) to my work, because there, mistakenly at the time, I thought I was running a business. There I learned the basics and, over time, advanced dentistry and doing what I like the most in dentistry: taking care of patients. I gained valuable experience in handling both surgically-difficult and psychologically-challenging cases. Nowadays, I see a lot of young, as well as not-so-young, dentists, who say they do only this treatment and do NOT do the rest of what they were taught in a dental school. They elect to fly to different States, where the pay is higher, but in a lot of cases, this limits their valuable learning experience to what we call "fill and drill." I met a lot of recent graduates who went through that experience, learning only how to restore dental fillings and low-quality crowns. It is like giving your car to a mechanic who only knows how to change tires, to fix a leak in the motor.

Without coming across as being immodest, I was then, and still am, a well-rounded dentist. Early on I also learned that patients appreciated having their dental needs met in one location. It is stressful enough for them to come into one dental office. They have no desire to go through that process again at a specialist's office at a different location.

Three years after finishing USC Dental School, I felt confident, and along with the experience I had gained, all prepared me to run my own office. A very modest two-chair dental office was my starting point. I was doing everything there myself. That is where I learned quickly that a dentist without a business person to manage the practice is just fifty percent of the equation. That is where I made the best investment in technology at the time: intraoral cameras had just come out on the market. It was a very brave move to purchase one at the time, as this equipment cost $5,000. It was a lot of money then. Now, similar equipment can be found for $300. That first camera served me well for years and I made my money back many times over. One can say that the ROI was immense.

The second best investment I made at the time was hiring our first business consultant. I recall thinking at the time the price to do that seemed like 'an arm and a leg' to me. But again, over time, it also proved to pay for itself many times over. I am now a big believer in business consultants services. ExecTech was most beneficial for me for many years. Scheduling Institute, another consulting company we hired, took me through the 2008 recession and helped to grow the business to where we are today. The main lesson I gained was: GIVE MORE VALUE IN SERVICES, THEN CHARGE FOR IT.

At the time I left the Anaheim practice, it had tripled in size. That was over 15 years ago, but I still miss the patients there. After being at a location one mile away for 7 years at our second practice, it was time to move to our present office. My wife and I had been looking at, and targeting, a particular building for several years. The building had a very inviting hallway and double doors to our suite. We had a vision. One of the things I have learned from Mike Dukes, one of my advisers at the time, is that *a move to a new location usually brings growth to the practice*. That's exactly what happened the first year, when we pulled the trigger on relocation. There were several reasons for it.

In his book *How to Win Friends and Influence People*, Andrew Carnegie recommends surrounding yourself with people who are smarter or more experienced – who, so to say, "have been there." Robert T. Kiyosaki echoes the same thoughts in *Rich Dad, Poor Dad*. He also stated that people who reached a certain status are more than willing to share their knowledge on the subject, partly because there is no value in it for them any longer. From early on, I have learned to get advice from such people. While reading Fred Joyal's *Marketing Is Everything*, where, among others, he mentioned Jay Geyer's Scheduling Institute. I was intrigued and hired Scheduling Institute for consulting services. Jay has always made a point that he is worth a fortune. He said that not to impress us, but to impress on us that advice is worth much more from a person who had already discovered the secret that there is no secret. There is just a better way doing things.

Steven R. Covey, in his bestseller, *The 7 Habits of Highly Effective People*, stated very clearly that a group of like-minded people will achieve a lot more than a single individual. To me, the best example of such cooperation was based on true events like the movie Miracle on Ice, when a bunch of college students beat the Russian Hockey National Team in Winter Olympics in Lake Placid in 1980. There were no stars on that American team, but the players were focused on one goal and one goal only: beat the Russians!

It is one thing is to watch the above story in the movie, it is another to live through a similar experience yourself. I want to share my personal experience during one of the training sessions at Benchmark Personal Growth Courses, in which I participated. One Thursday night, a group of us, strangers who had met for the first time the night before, were faced with what seemed like an impossible task for ALL of us. Just two days later, that disorganized group worked like a well-oiled machine. What was seen as impossible a very short time ago, was accomplished in triumph. The positive energy we experienced during that exercise, working together, is hard to describe. When we looked at each other during the last part of the exercise, knowing we figured out the puzzle placed in front of us, one could see that nothing could stop us! It just took alignment and desire to succeed *consistently*.

Those values I learned at Benchmark, I instill in people I work with at the office. Always looking to improve performance by sharing my life experiences and earning the trust of patients, when compared to my last practice, we tripled the size of the present one. The move was justified.

Dentistry is a tough business. One has to love what he does. Otherwise, hearing "I hate dentists" on a regular basis is discouraging, to say the least. Focusing on getting people out of pain and misery, changing their lives with smile makeovers, and staying on course is the only way to make it work. What helped was to learn a concept called WIN-WIN-WIN,[1] which became a philosophy of life for me, and one which I teach and share with friends, patients and staff alike.

Even though I am a great dentist, I cannot do it alone. My caring and friendly coworkers and I create a synergy to deliver the best dental care to our wonderful patients. And even though I do not always express it, I feel immensely grateful to be so lucky to do what I do and deliver.

Acknowledgment to:

Lilian Thriling, who instilled a confidence in me at a time when it was most needed.

Carol Snow, who was instrumental in making my dream come true.

My wife, Inna, who is my biggest critic, for supporting my decisions every day.

My son, Ron, who continues "tradition," legacy, if you will. Love you very much.

---

1. The WIN-WIN-WIN concept is very simple. The customer, the company and its employees must all win in any one transaction.

About Dr. Michael

Dr. Ayzin has been in private practice for over 25 years. He studied Psychobiology at the University of Southern California and due to rapid acceleration in his studies, he earned his DDS Degree at USC Dental School in 1988. Dr. Ayzin is a Fellow of The World Clinical Laser & Imaging (WCLI) Institute. He is affiliated with the American Academy of Cosmetic Dentistry, Academy of General Dentistry, American Dental Association, California Dental Association, and Orange County Dental Society. He is also on HOAG staff, one of the best hospitals in Orange County.

Dr. Ayzin specializes in state-of-the-art cosmetic treatments, including porcelain veneers, and full mouth reconstruction, as well as fast and effective relief of pain, repairing broken and chipped teeth, tooth-colored dental fillings, root canals, wisdom tooth and other difficult tooth extractions, periodontal care for bleeding gums and geriatric dentistry.

A very large spectrum of his practice is fearful patients who were afraid of dental work for years. In conjunction with a group of well-qualified anesthesiologists, Dr. Ayzin treats these patients very successfully under complete or IV sedation. Patients love to have this option available to them.

Dr. Ayzin has been happily married for 28 years and has a son. Besides loving dentistry, he enjoys traveling, fishing, and photography.

CHAPTER 21

MINDSET AND FULFILLMENT ARE THE KEY INGREDIENTS OF SUCCESS

BY RICHARD BUETTNER

There are two lakes in Israel, The Sea of Galilee and The Dead Sea. Both lakes are attached to and fed by the Jordan River. The Sea of Galilee is fed by the Jordan River which feeds it back to the river. The Sea of Galilee is the lake that nourishes most of Israel, it is filled with life, and in turn, gives life to many. It is Israel's largest freshwater lake and absolutely picturesque. Throughout history, towns and cities have been situated on the Sea, and it has served as a center of trade. Fish and plant life are abundant in the area. Today, the Sea of Galilee is just as active and populated as a regional center of commerce and tourism, and is surrounded by farms, resorts and bustling communities.

The Dead Sea, on the other hand, is also fed by the Jordan River, but the water of The Dead Sea goes nowhere. The Dead Sea does not feed anything, and it keeps all the water it is given. The Dead Sea is barren and lifeless. In it, no life survives. Though the beautiful aqua water of the Dead Sea resembles parts of the Caribbean, looks can surely be deceiving. You see — there are absolutely no plants, no fish, and no visible life present in the Dead Sea due to its extreme salinity. The Dead Sea extracts life but gives none. Its only real benefit is as a giant salt reserve and raw source for various skin treatment products.

As stated above, both the Sea of Galilee and the Dead Sea are fed by the Jordan River. There is really only one difference between these two bodies of water, only one thing that causes the Sea of Galilee to be beautiful and alive while the Dead Sea is barren and lifeless. The difference is that the Sea of Galilee takes water from the Jordan River, and then gives back water to the river. The water simply passes through. As a result, the Sea of Galilee is full of life and beauty. The Dead Sea, on the other hand, only takes water, but gives nothing back, and as a result it sustains no life. Those two bodies of water bear witness to a truth of human life. It is in receiving and then giving back that life and hope are sustained. In other words, The Sea of Galilee is a conduit, The Dead Sea is a container. The first is full of life, the second is full of death!

Life works the same way. Your greatness is not about what you have. It's about what you give. Whether it's being generous with your words, time or money – when we lose ourselves in generosity, we discover the true meaning of happiness! The same is true in our spiritual life. If you and I have spiritual input but no spiritual output, we will become stagnant, lifeless, bitter, and caustic. However, if we, like the Sea of Galilee, are receiving and giving back, we become vibrant, healthy and life-giving.

GIVE LOVE TODAY! IT'S GOOD FOR THE SOUL!

I come from a very humble background. I grew up in a small village with all my family trading their time for money, and I always dreamed of having an abundant life—a life filled with health, wealth, love and happiness. I dreamed of traveling the world, having friends in every single country, giving people inspiration, and being able to care for my family and my future family. Seeing my family work 60, 70 or even 80+ hours a week without creating a lifestyle they desired was really discouraging. I knew there must be something different.

In school, I was thinking that if I really became great at this going to school, getting good grades and finding a job thing, that my life would look like that, or like the life of my teachers or my friends' parents. Now, I don't even want to be great at that.

In life you can choose between two paths:

1. Do what everybody else does. Tell everyone you don't care about money yet spend most of your life working for money.

-- Or --

2. You can choose to build a purpose-driven lifestyle.

When I was stuck in that first path, my entire focus was on how to get out of that. This almost got me kicked out of my job.

--I felt like a failure.
--My personality changed.
--I became super-shy and introverted.
--I was scared to speak about my deep thoughts and emotions. I was not even able to speak in front of my school class, because I was so focused on what everybody else thought of me.

I've never been the smartest kid in school, yet I knew if something excites me, I'm ALL IN and able to achieve greatness. That's when I realized it was not me who was the failure. This system is just not made for everybody.

In life, you can either have your circumstances define your future OR you can design your future by redefining your circumstances.

Your perception of how you view a specific situation is essential. If you have a roof over your head, a bed to sleep in, electricity, access to fresh water, 2-3 meals a day, education and enough money to buy this book, you have more resources than 70-80% of the population on this planet. Realize that and be grateful.

I've always been inspired by people who did what they love. There's nothing more contagious than someone who is truly aligned with their long term vision. Passion, excitement and high energy were the attributes I was seeking.

From my background playing professional basketball, I knew the best way to get what you want is by following your idols, role models, and MENTORS.

If you feel the same way I did, just remember one thing:

In the end, everything is beautiful,
If it's not beautiful, it's not the end.

Also, never forget:

Big people fall, small people rise,
You never know when it's your time.

I started reading books about the Law of Attraction, and I read *Rich Dad, Poor Dad* by Robert Kiyosaki, which completely blew my mind. I started attracting the right people, the right opportunities and this time I was ready.

Enough of watching other people live their dream life on YouTube, Facebook or Instagram. First it starts as a dream, then comes some faith. The moment you build your belief, everything changes. I got to know my mentor Jonathan from Hollywood, Los Angeles, teaching me his mind mastery of manifesting anything I wanted.

Not just the amount of opportunities around us determine if we become successful at this game called life. It's the number of opportunities we take for granted that decides between success and failure, health and sickness, happiness and depression.

Growing up, I was a very shy and introverted person, and the people I spent a lot of time with knew that. Everything is a blessing and a curse at the same time. Our perception and judgement give situations their meaning and opinions. I didn't like being shy. I hated not being able to communicate what was on my mind. I wanted to have more courage. Later on, I realized that this made me OBSERVE people. You can only connect the dots backwards, so that's why reflecting on the past is important. Reflect in a completely neutral manner without too much emotion to find the nuggets/lessons, what to continue and what to improve from now on.

Observing others helped me understand people and most importantly myself. The goal is not to become rich but happy. Once your own energy level is high enough you will attract other high level people and others will naturally feel drawn to you. Then, you just need a product to share and serve these people. Financial abundance, which we all define differently, follows once we move in the right direction with the right intention.

As we grow older, we also grow wiser. Finding out what you desire and carefully mapping out how you see your life in the future will separate you from 99% of those on this planet. I have seen countless people walk through life without a clear understanding of what makes them fulfilled. So, obviously, not knowing where you want to go will lead you nowhere. To put this into perspective, it is like driving a car into the middle of nowhere without a GPS in foggy weather, and you cannot see more than 50 to 100 meters ahead.

The intentions of your heart will lead you to your destination like the GPS in your car. Even if you can only see the next 50 to 100 meters ahead, you trust your GPS. In the same way, trusting your intuition will lead you to a blessed life even if you can only see the next few steps. Trust and knowing that everything will be beautiful is the core essence for so many people living extraordinary lives.

Here are the 8 Rules for Fulfillment.

1. MAKE PEACE WITH YOUR PAST. That way, it will not disturb your present, which manifests the future.
2. WHAT OTHER PEOPLE THINK OF YOU IS NONE OF YOUR BUSINESS.
3. TIME HEALS ALMOST EVERYTHING. Give it time.
4. NO ONE IS IN CHARGE OF YOUR HAPPINESS. Except YOU!
5. DO NOT COMPARE YOUR LIFE TO OTHERS and don't judge them. You have no idea what their journey is all about.
6. STOP THINKING TOO MUCH. It's all right not to know all the answers. They will come to you when you least expect it and let go.
7. SMILE. You don't own all the problems in the world.
8. LOVE YOURSELF AND THE PEOPLE AROUND YOU.

The difference between people who live a fulfilled life and those who are unfulfilled is self-realization. Success is not everything.

Philosophies of Life – Living full and dying empty

-- What matters in the end is what matters most to you. If you value spending time with loved ones more than achieving something of greater public value to the world, then I would suggest you follow your desires.

-- To truly control your destiny, you need to understand not only the world around you, but also the world within you.

-- Let us not forget that there is always a way to have it all, to find the balance between things. If you cannot see where the balance lies, it is only because you've yet to obtain enough wisdom to see it.

-- Work toward making yourself better and the answer will appear. The answer is there, but you must raise your frequency enough, through acceptance and understanding, to see it.

-- There are way too many books that have never been written, songs that have never been sung and companies that have never been built because the fear of failure was bigger than somebody's desire to make this world a better place.

-- Sacrifice who you have been in the past to become the shining light that is dormant inside of you.

Most people play to lose small. We play to win big.

1. Seek truth over everything.
2. Life is about improving and enriching the lives of others, money will follow.
3. Systems beat intelligence.
4. Eliminating is often more important than adding.
5. Real change only happens when it is reached by one's own effort.
6. Think big and be willing to entertain anything, even if it puts into question everything you have believed up to this point prior.

Why not live life to the fullest and enjoy the flowers life has to offer? Do not be scared to make that change. For every big shift in our society, every person that changed the paradigm of humanity had to overcome this. Lose yourself in your purpose and automatically you have no time to worry about what could go wrong. Have patience on your rise up the ladder, and stay humble once you made it to the top.

Big people fall, small people rise,
You never know when it's your time.

Yet your time will come.

Factuality < Actuality

Looking back on my life, there was no way for me to achieve all these amazing things.

- Traveling the world 24/7.
- Impacting millions of people in all areas of life.
- Having a wonderful, loving family, friends and business partners around me.
- Building businesses with over ten million dollars in revenue before I turned 24.
- I am giving back to those that matter the most: my loved ones, people that deserve it and everybody else who has no one else to help them.

This was a long shot.

Looking at the facts:

-- Growing up in a small town in one of the poorest areas of my country. More obstacles than opportunities. Nobody is believing in you or themselves.
-- Dropping out of high school to be independent financially and make ends meet.

That was my reality. Yet I realized that the perception of reality is greater than reality itself. Learning this from my mentor Jonathan Amaret and applying it to get out from thousands of €uros in debt at age 21, to retiring and living the dream ever since I turned 23.

Make sure you do not compare your life path to anybody else's. Your journey is incomparable to anyone before and after you. Yes, there are people who understand you but nobody will ever know the whole story as well as you. Be patient on your way and understand that the bigger the dream, the longer it can take to manifest it.

Once you achieve whatever you perceive as success, your attitude determines how high you go and how long you stay there.

> *Big people fall and small people rise,*
> *You never know when it is your time.*

We aren't motivated by our dreams but by what we least accept for ourselves. So, raise your standards. Don't settle for that "B" life!

Imagine your (future) wife/husband is watching you whatever you do.

How to transform your life:

1. The easiest way to transform your life is by transforming yourself.
2. The easiest way to transform yourself is by transforming reality/light/everything that is and will be.
3. The easiest way to transform light is by transforming gravity.
4. The easiest way to transform gravity is by transforming your thoughts.
5. The easiest way to transform your thoughts is by transforming your feelings.
6. The easiest way to transform your feelings is by ACCEPTING the past, present   and future.
7. The easiest way to ACCEPT what's going on in Life is by realizing that you are everything and everybody that was, is and will be.

You are THE SOURCE!

You DECIDE what happens in Your Life!

You are not just a drop in the ocean,
You are the entire OCEAN in a drop.

When people think about traveling to the past, they worry about accidentally changing the present, but no one in the present really thinks they can radically change the future.

BE THE CHANGE WE ALL SO DESPERATELY NEED!

One person can't change the world, yet we can all create the impact and ripple effect by changing one life at a time. Real change can only come from within so do not worry about anybody else's change but yours.

Be the change you want to see in this world. We are in a big shift of wisdom and fulfillment. Now is the time to take charge of your life, for the sake of yourself, your family, the people around you and the rest of us celebrating your breakthroughs.

Dream Big Dreams because small dreams have no magic. You've got to follow your passion. You've got to figure out what it is you love. So, figure out who you really are. And have the courage to do that. I believe that the only courage anybody ever needs is the courage to follow your own dreams. In a limitless world, anything is possible.

You are the co creator of your own life, world and universe. Use the power you've been given since birth to take control and build your personal legacy. Life is all about the moment of now and the memories you share with your loved ones.

Become the best version of yourself and be an example for the rest of us to follow.

About Richard

Richard Buettner (b. June 14, 1994) is a German Entrepreneur, Visionary and Brand Strategist. He is a pioneer in the influencer marketing and affiliate marketing scene in Germany and his organization brings in millions of dollars in revenue a year.

Richard grew up in Egeln, Germany and has always had a competitive nature. An athlete, Richard played soccer in his youth but later switched to playing basketball as a teenager. He would later play basketball in California at Merced High School and Mitteldeutscher Basketball Club (MBC) in the 1st German Basketball League when he was 16 years old. Although his parents were separated, they were both entrepreneurs in their own life. He credits his mom with teaching him how to cultivate a business mindset but also instilling compassion in him. When he was 16, he was introduced to the Law of Attraction/Vibration and utilized it for his future success.

He dropped out of school in 11th grade and started a sales job in his native Germany. When he was 20 years old, he switched to online marketing and joined a high-end nutrition company, becoming one of the first to utilize social media marketing for his success. For this company, he built a team of 400 people, becoming the top leader in all of East Germany.

In January 2016, Richard partnered with a financial education company based in the USA, and served as the President of the organization in Europe. He recruited a team of over 2,000 active distributors generating millions of dollars in sales.

2018 was his absolute breakthrough year, becoming a self-made millionaire at age 24 and helping the biggest Forex and crypto-trading education platform company to explode in Europe and all over the world. In addition, he built a huge social media brand and fan base reaching millions of people.

Richard is producing some of the most watched travel lifestyle videos working with some of the biggest names in the world — from celebrity artists like David Guetta to the most powerful entertainment brands like Marvel.

Now in 2019, he is launching a global movement with impactful influencers from different industries empowering people to become the best version of themselves.

The mission is to create a better world around us starting with ourselves. He believes we should give an opportunity to those who deserve it by helping millions around the globe with their health, wealth, love and happiness.